Movie Clips For Kids

Faith-Building Video Devotions

Group
Loveland, Colorado

Group's R.E.A.L. Guarantee to you:

Every Group resource incorporates our R.E.A.L. approach to ministry—
a unique philosophy that results in long-term retention and life
transformation. It's ministry that's:

**This is EARL.
He's R.E.A.L.
mixed up.
(Get it?)**

Relational
Because student-to-
student interaction
enhances learning and
builds Christian
friendships.

Experiential
Because what students
experience sticks with
them up to 9 times
longer than what they
simply hear or read.

Applicable
Because the aim of
Christian education is
to be both hearers and
doers of the Word.

Learner-based
Because students learn
more and retain it
longer when the
process is designed
according to how they
learn best.

Movie Clips for Kids: Faith-Building Video Devotions
Copyright © 2002 Group Publishing, Inc.

Visit our Web site: **www.grouppublishing.com**

Credits
Contributing Authors: Teryl Cartwright, Diane Cory, Ruthie Daniels, Heather A. Eades, Sheila Halasz,
Laure Herlinger, Jan Kershner, Becca Koopmans, Julie Lavender, Jennifer Nystrom, Chris Perciante,
Pamela Shoup, Alex Shallenberger, Larry Shallenberger, Gary Troutman, and Courtney Wright
Editor: Karl Leuthauser
Chief Creative Officer: Joani Schultz
Art Director: Sharon Anderson
Computer Graphic Artist: Stephen Beer
Illustrator: Patty O'Friel
Cover Art Director: Jeff A. Storm
Cover Illustrator: Patty O'Friel
Cover Designer: Alan Furst Inc
Production Manager: DeAnne Lear

ISBN 0-7644-2383-5
Printed in the United States of America.

10 9 8 7 6 5 4 3 2 1   11 10 09 08 07 06 05 04 03 02

CONTENTS

INTRODUCTION

"**L**ast week, we brought in a gospel illusionist. The week before, our drama team did a puppet production for the entire hour. Next week, I'm hiring a clown and renting a cotton candy maker. Every week, I have to do more and more to keep the kids' attention. I just can't compete with Hollywood."

We are competing for the hearts and minds of our children. So much in this world calls for and captures their attention. Unfortunately, many of the messages behind the production and special effects do not honor God or edify the souls of our kids.

We can work ourselves to death to create a Christian production every Sunday that will keep kids interested. Or...we can use the very thing that captures their attention to teach them the most important lessons and to help children grow in their faith. Instead of competing with Hollywood, we can use it as a tool to advance the kingdom of God.

Have you ever noticed how just turning on the television commands the attention of children? Even when they're watching snow as you rewind the movie, children watch in an almost hypnotic state. What's even more amazing is that they remember what they see. Ask a child about his or her favorite movie, and you'll hear the entire plot, the lessons learned, and many of the lines word for word.

What an opportunity we have! If the television creates a captive audience, why not help that audience learn about Jesus? *Movie Clips for Kids* offers **one hundred clips** you can use to teach at least fifty different Bible stories to your kids. And every clip offers an exciting active learning experience. That way, you don't have to go from a captivating clip to a boring lecture. Instead, you can move from an interesting clip straight to a fun activity that reinforces your point.

Are you looking for something to supplement your Sunday school lesson and give some extra pizazz? Go to the Table of Contents to find just about every major Bible story you'll teach this year. Maybe you need some help teaching children about an important topic? Check out the topical index in the back of the book. Find your topic, grab your movie, and you're ready to go!

The production has already been done for you with multimillion dollar budgets. You can captivate and interest children without spending a bundle or burning out your staff. So pop the popcorn, load the VCR, and get ready to change the world for Christ!

Oh yeah...a couple of important things before you begin. For the most part, federal copyright laws do not allow you to use videos (even ones you own) for any purpose other than home viewing. Though some exceptions allow for the use of short segments of copyrighted material for educational purposes, it's best to be on the safe side. Your church can obtain a license from the Motion Picture Licensing Corporation for a small fee that covers video use for the whole church. Just visit www.mplc.com or call 1-800-462-8855 for more information.

We've also asked our authors to work hard to keep the video segments wholesome and appropriate for children's ministry. You'll notice that most of the clips are rated G and a few are PG. But that doesn't guarantee that you or someone in your church won't find the clip offensive. **Make sure you watch the clip before you show it to the children in your ministry.**

You also have to remember that **children may see your showing of the clip as an endorsement of the whole movie.** While the clip may be perfectly innocent, a child may go home excitedly and say, "Guess what we watched at church today?" The parents may rent the movie and call you the next day saying, "I can't believe you let my child watch that movie! Do you know what happens in the movie? Our pastor is going to hear about this!" The parent may be overreacting. The parent may have a good point. Either way, parents have a right to protect their children. So you may want to let parents know that you're planning on using movie clips, how you'll use them, and why you're using them before you begin. It seems as if just about every high-budget production has *something* in it that *someone* may object to, so be sensitive. **Just because you think the movie is OK doesn't mean parents will.** We've included a letter and movie announcement on pages 7-8 that you can use to communicate with parents. You can photocopy the pages and send them out or adjust them to meet your needs.

I think that covers the basics. Now sit back and enjoy the show!

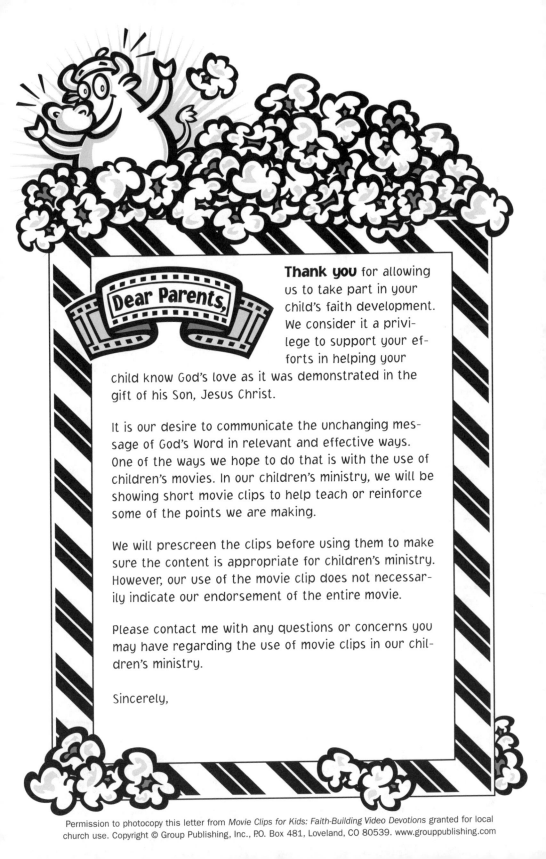

Dear Parents,

Thank you for allowing us to take part in your child's faith development. We consider it a privilege to support your efforts in helping your child know God's love as it was demonstrated in the gift of his Son, Jesus Christ.

It is our desire to communicate the unchanging message of God's Word in relevant and effective ways. One of the ways we hope to do that is with the use of children's movies. In our children's ministry, we will be showing short movie clips to help teach or reinforce some of the points we are making.

We will prescreen the clips before using them to make sure the content is appropriate for children's ministry. However, our use of the movie clip does not necessarily indicate our endorsement of the entire movie.

Please contact me with any questions or concerns you may have regarding the use of movie clips in our children's ministry.

Sincerely,

On _____,

our children's ministry will show a short clip

from the movie _____

_____

as a tool to teach children about _____

_____

_____

_____.

Attention Parents!

Please let us know if you have
any questions or concerns.

Thank you!

On _____,

our children's ministry will show a short clip

from the movie _____

_____

as a tool to teach children about _____

_____

_____

_____.

Attention Parents!

Please let us know if you have
any questions or concerns.

Thank you!

CREATION

IT'S A SMALL WORLD • *Scripture: Genesis 1:1–2:3*

Movie Title:
🎥 HONEY, I SHRUNK THE KIDS (PG)

Start Time: 18 minutes, 15 seconds

Where to Begin: The kids realize they've been shrunk in size, swept up, and put out with the trash.

The Critics Say

Use this clip to teach children about the wonder of the world God created, trust, friendship, or God's protection.

Where to End: About a minute later, they head off into the "wilderness."

Plot: During a family scientific experiment gone awry, a group of neighborhood kids are shrunk to the size of small insects. They suddenly find themselves deep within the grass of the back yard, which now looks gigantic and unfamiliar.

Review: You can use this scene to help children look at God's incredible creation in a new and fresh way. Kids and adults alike are prone to take for granted the amazing world God has given us, focusing instead on our own day-to-day concerns. But this movie clip can help children look past the obvious and discover anew the wonder and intricacy of the world God has set before us. By identifying with the kids in the movie, who suddenly see their world from a completely different perspective, the kids in your class can also undergo a shift in thinking that will stay with them long after class.

Supplies: Newsprint, tape, markers, and crayons

Preshow: On a wall, hang a large sheet of newsprint for every three students in class. Make sure the newsprint is at kids' eye level. Set out markers and crayons near each sheet. Have kids form groups of three.

now PLAYING

Say➔ Today we're going to talk about God's amazing creation of the world. We're surrounded by the cool things God made. But sometimes we get so used to seeing God's creation around us that we don't really pay attention to it. In this movie clip from *Honey, I Shrunk the Kids,* a group of kids suddenly sees creation in a whole new way. Let's watch.

Show the *Honey, I Shrunk the Kids* clip.

Ask➔ • How do you think those kids felt when they realized how little they were?
• How did their perspective of God's creation change?
• What do you think surprised them most about their new situation?

Say➔ The familiar back yard suddenly seemed new and amazing to these kids because they were seeing it from a different viewpoint. Let's have each group move to a sheet of newsprint hanging on the wall. On your group's newsprint, work together to draw a picture of a part of creation. But here's the catch.

You have to draw it from a new perspective. Maybe you'll draw it from the perspective of being really small, as in our movie clip. Or maybe you'll draw it from the perspective of a bird flying high above. It's up to you. You'll have five minutes.

Call time after five minutes, then let each group display and explain its drawing. After each presentation, lead kids in a round of applause.

Ask→ • **How was drawing a favorite part of creation from a new perspective like what the kids in the movie experienced?**
• **How can seeing God's creation in new ways help you praise him more?**
• **What can you do this week to view God's creation as fresh and exciting?**

DON'T FLUB IT UP! • Scripture: Genesis 1:1–2:3

Movie Title:
FLUBBER (PG)

Start Time: 10 minutes, 50 seconds

Where to Begin: Flubber is first created.

Where to End: Not quite two minutes later, the professor has enjoyed Flubber's many qualities, but before Flubber becomes frightened and flies away.

> The Critics Say
>
> You can also use this movie clip to teach children about God's creativity, their self-worth as God's children, or becoming new creations in Christ.

Plot: Professor Philip Brainard is an absent-minded scientist who even forgets his own wedding day as he tries to create flying rubber, or Flubber. Just as he starts to walk away in defeat, thinking he has failed yet again, he hears something percolating in his pressure-cooker. He opens the lid and—much to his surprise—finds Flubber! The amazing qualities of this new substance amaze and delight the professor.

Review: This movie clip provides a great way to introduce kids to the surprising and exciting nature of God's creation. While the invention of Flubber in this clip was accidental, it was still a delightful revelation. How much more delightful and amazing, then, is God's intentional and perfect creation. Use this clip to help kids see and appreciate the miracle of God's creation.

Supplies: A ball of modeling dough or clay for each child

NOW PLAYING

Have kids sit in a circle on the floor.

Say→ Let's talk a little about God's creation. We'll play a quick game of I Spy as we go around the circle. Each person will name one part of God's creation that he or she can see from the circle. You can name an obvious part of creation, such as the sun or trees, or you can name a less obvious part of creation. For example, you could say, "I spy a pencil, which is made of wood, which is made from trees that God created." Try not to repeat what anyone else has said. Ready? Let's play!

Go around the circle several times or until kids run out of ideas.

Say→ God made so many new and amazing things!

Ask→ • What do you think it would be like to create something brand new— something that had never been seen before?

Say→ I have a movie clip to show you about the invention of something new. Let's watch a scene from the movie *Flubber*.

Show the *Flubber* clip.

Ask→ • How did the professor react when he invented Flubber?
• How is that like or unlike the way you think God reacted with each new creation he made?

Say→ The inventor of Flubber was surprised at his creation. But God knew exactly what he was doing every time he created something. God was still happy with his creations. In fact, the Bible tells us that he said everything he made was "good." Let's do a little creating ourselves!

Give each child a ball of modeling dough or clay. Explain to kids that they will have a few minutes to each create a totally new thing or person. Ask each child to name his or her creation and think of three characteristics it possesses. After a few minutes, call time. Let each child present his or her creation. After the kids have shared their creations, lead the class in a round of applause for everyone's participation.

Ask→ • How did you feel when you finished making your new creation?
• How do you think God feels about each of *his* creations?
• How do you think God feels about you?

Say→ God made everything in the universe and declared it "good." And God made each of us. In fact, it wasn't until he had made humans that he declared his creation "very good." Each one of us is a special creation made by God, but we all have something in common. The Bible tells us that God made us in his image, which means that we really are special creations made by the master inventor himself!

THE FALL

WE'VE GOT TROUBLE! • Scripture: Genesis 3:1-24

 Movie Title:
THE MUSIC MAN (NOT RATED)

Start Time: 10 minutes, 9 seconds

Where to Begin: The professor begins to sing "Ya Got Trouble (Right Here in River City)."

Use this clip to teach children about temptation, discernment, or obedience.

Where to End: Almost two minutes later, the "Ya Got Trouble" segment ends.

Plot: Professor Harold Hill gathers together the townspeople of River City, a small town in Iowa, to warn them of the dangers that abound with the addition of a pool table.

Review: Use this clip to help children see that there are those who know more than they do about what is good and what is harmful for them. While the professor in this movie has his own motives for warning the people of River City about temptation, the scene can be useful in leading into a discussion about the topic of temptation and where to turn to avoid temptation.

Supplies: Paper and pencils

NOW PLAYING

Have children form groups of three or four. Give each group a sheet of paper and a pencil.

Ask→ • What does the word *temptation* mean?

• Has anyone here ever been tempted to do something wrong? Let's see a show of hands.

Say→ We're all tempted to sin, or do wrong things, at times. And being tempted to sin goes back all the way to the Garden of Eden, when Adam and Eve were tempted to disobey God and eat the forbidden fruit. Unfortunately, they gave in to the temptation, and people have been sinning ever since. But God had warned Adam and Eve not to eat the forbidden fruit; he warned them not to give in to temptation.

I have a movie clip here that shows Professor Hill warning others about temptation. It's a scene from a musical called *The Music Man.* Let's see what he says about temptation.

Show the clip from *The Music Man.*

Ask→ • Why do you think Professor Hill was trying so hard to warn others about temptation?

• Who warns you to stay away from temptation?

Say→ With your group members, think about wrongs things that kids your age are tempted to do. Have someone in your group write a list of your ideas on your sheet of paper.

Give kids a few minutes to write their ideas. Then let each group share its list with the rest of the class.

Say→ Now look at your list, and choose one of the temptations you wrote. Turn your paper over, and work together to come up with a rhyme that talks about that temptation. Try to make your rhyme sound like the one you heard in the movie. So you might say, "We've got *trouble,* right here in [name of your town]. That starts with T and that rhymes with C and that means no *cheating*!"

Walk around the room to offer encouragement and help as needed. After a few minutes, let each group shout out its rhyme. Then gather children together.

Ask→ • **What do you do when you're tempted to do something wrong?**
• **How can you resist temptations when they come your way?**

I WANT MORE! • Scripture: Genesis 3:1-24

Movie Title:
THE LITTLE MERMAID (G)

Start Time: 11 minutes, 30 seconds

Where to Begin: Ariel sings a song about wanting more out of life than her father is willing to permit.

You could use this movie clip to teach children about obedience, God's provision, rebellion, or the consequences of sin.

Where to End: Ariel ends her song.

Plot: Ariel, a young mermaid, has been sternly warned by her father, King Triton, not to swim to the surface of the ocean. He has tried to warn her of the dangers and consequences of such an action, but Ariel can only think of her own wishes.

Review: You can use this scene from the movie to help kids understand temptation and the importance of obedience. Adam and Eve had everything they needed or could possibly want in the Garden of Eden. But they gave in to the temptation of evil and wanted just a little bit more, even though God had expressly forbidden eating the fruit offered by the serpent. Children will easily be able to make the connection between Ariel disobeying her father's instructions and Adam and Eve disobeying their heavenly Father.

NOW PLAYING

Say→ Let's start our time together with a quick game. Our game is like Mother May I. But today, we'll call it Father May I. Does everyone know how to play? As we play, you'll need to pay attention to what I say because the game will have a few twists and turns in it. Ready? Let's play!

Explain to kids that they will form pairs and link arms with their partners. Pairs will line up next to each other at one end of the room. You'll stand at the other end, and point at random to a pair of children. Give the pair verbal instructions such as "Take one giant step forward" or "Jump up and down three times." Partners should obey your commands only after they ask, in unison, "Father, may I?" Then they must obey the instruction together. Explain that if partners forget to ask "Father, may I?" or fail to follow the instruction together, the pair is out of the game.

Quickly point to each pair of kids, and give instructions rapidly. Continue this fast-paced game until all the pairs are out of the game or until one pair successfully reaches you. If you have time, play more rounds of the game by letting children take turns being the leader. After the game, gather everyone together.

Ask→ • What happened in this game when you forgot to ask permission?
• What kinds of things do you ask permission for in real life?

Say→ It's important to ask our parents and teachers for permission before we do things. They don't give us permission to do things that would hurt us or wouldn't be good for us. But sometimes we disobey. Let's watch a movie clip from *The Little Mermaid*. In this clip, Ariel, the little mermaid, thinks about disobeying *her* father.

Play the clip from *The Little Mermaid*.

Ask→ • Why didn't Ariel want to obey her father?
• Think about a time you disobeyed your parents. What happened?

Say→ Sometimes when we disobey, our parents have to punish us. It's kind of like what happened in Father, May I? when we took a step without permission and then had to sit out of the game.

That's a lot like what happened to Adam and Eve in the Bible. God gave them one rule to obey—not to eat from one particular tree in the Garden. But they disobeyed, so God punished them by sending them out of the Garden, sort of like the way you were sent out of the game.

Ask→ • How do you think Ariel's father felt when she disobeyed?
• How do you think God felt when Adam and Eve disobeyed him?
• How do you think God feels when we disobey him?

Say→ God loves us and wants only what's best for us. His rules are perfect. Let's all to try to obey God this week and always!

Have children stand in a circle with you. Turn to a child next to you, shake hands and say, "Say you'll obey!" Then have the child pass the phrase and handshake to the next person in the circle, and so on until the handshake comes back to you.

THE FLOOD

A FLOATING ZOO • Scripture: *Genesis 6:9–8:22*

Movie Title:
FREE WILLY (PG)

You could use this clip to teach children about God's provision, wisdom, and plans.

The Critics Say

Start Time: 33 minutes, 37 seconds

Where to Begin: Jesse's showing off Willy's newly learned skills for the owner and manager of the adventure park.

Where to End: Willy ends his performance.

Plot: Jesse, a troubled young boy in a new foster family, has been working at the Northwest Adventure Park as a way to make up for some bad behavior. At the park, Willy (the orca whale) has been display-ing some bad behavior of his own. Caught by a whale catcher and put in the park to perform and draw in customers, Willy has re-fused to be trained. The park's owner refuses to pay for a bigger tank for Willy and has even hinted at getting rid of him. But Jesse and Willy hit it off, and Jesse is the only one to whom Willy re-sponds. Jesse has been able to train Willy and is showing off Willy's skills for the owner and manager.

Review: Use this scene to remind children that God cares about every living creature—humans and animals alike. God had plans before the Flood to save Noah and his family and every kind of animal on the earth. In Free Willy, a lonely young boy and a lonely whale meet and find a relationship that helps them both. Jesse goes to a lot of trouble to help Willy and save his future. In the same way, God went to extraordinary means to ensure the survival of each kind of animal during the Flood.

Supplies: Clean, clear plastic deli containers with lids; clean, foam meat trays; scissors; markers; string; tape; and water (Check with your local grocery store for the deli containers and foam meat trays. They're usually available for a very minimal charge.)

Preshow: Cut a 3x4-inch foam rectangle for each child in class. Then make a one-inch cut inward toward the center from each corner. If you have a number of young children in class, you may want to tape the "arks" to-gether beforehand. Also cut a four-inch length of string for each child.

NOW PLAYING

Say→ Today we're going to watch a clip from the movie *Free Willy*. It's about a whale named Willy who's in danger of being kicked out of the adventure park where he lives. Willy hasn't responded to his new surroundings and hasn't lived up to his new owner's expectations. In fact, Willy's in danger of being done away with if he doesn't start performing tricks for the crowds. But you'll see that there's someone who's willing to help save Willy. Let's watch.

Show the clip from *Free Willy*.

Ask→ • How do you think Willy felt when he realized he was in danger?
• What might have happened if Jesse hadn't helped Willy?

Say→ Jesse helped Willy because he cared about him. When God decided to send the Flood to the earth, he cared about Noah and his family and about the animals. In fact, God saved two of every kind of animal in the whole world!

God directed Noah to build an ark, which was a big boat. It had to be a re-ally big boat because it had to hold all those animals! Let's make some arks of our own.

Demonstrate how to fold up the sides of the foam rectangles you pre-pared before class, and tape the sides together to form the sides of an

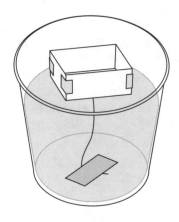

"ark." (Tell kids not to worry if the edges don't exactly meet—the ark will float anyway!) Give kids each a length of string, and have kids tape one end of the string to the bottom of their ark, and the other end of the string to the inside bottom of a deli container.

Set out colorful markers for kids to share. Have kids draw fish and other underwater creatures around the outside of the deli containers. (Encourage kids to draw Willy, too!) When kids are finished drawing, pour a small amount of water into each container before covering securely with the lid.

Have kids take their ark crafts home with them and use them to tell their family members and friends how God saved the animals during the Flood!

The Critics Say

For extra fun, give kids a few gummy bears to place in their arks.

WHAT DID YOU SAY? • Scripture: Genesis 6:9–8:22

Movie Title:
HOMEWARD BOUND: THE INCREDIBLE JOURNEY (1993) (G)

Start Time: 16 minutes, 50 seconds

Where to Begin: Chance, Shadow, and Sassy reach the crest of a mountain near the start of their journey.

The Critics Say

Use this clip to teach children about God's provision and protection.

Where to End: About a minute later, after they discuss whether to continue on.

Plot: Two dogs, Chance and Shadow, and Sassy, the cat, are afraid they've been abandoned by their family, so they set out on a lengthy journey home. In this scene, near the start of their journey, they discuss what the best course of action is in their situation.

Review: This clip can help children relate to the Bible story of the Flood in a childlike and nonthreatening way. After all, the destruction of the world and almost everything in it can be scary to kids! By introducing the story with this clip of talking animals and then letting children use their imaginations to think about what the animals on the ark might have said to each other, you can teach the Bible story and the truths it contains in a way that can minimize kids' fears.

Supplies: Paper and pencils

now PLAYING

Say→ We're going to watch a scene from *Homeward Bound.* Two dogs named Chance and Shadow and a cat named Sassy are afraid of being separated from their family forever. So they decide to set out on their own to find their way home. Along the way, they stop to talk. Let's watch.

Show the *Homeward Bound* clip.

Ask→
- **What could you tell about the personalities of the dogs and cat by the things they said?**
- **Which animal did you like best? Why?**
- **Do you think that animals ever communicate with each other? Explain.**

Distribute paper and pencils.

Say:→ Let's think for a minute about the animals on the ark that Noah built. Think of one animal that was on the ark. Then write on your paper what that animal might have said to the animal next to it just as God closed the door of the ark.

Give kids a few minutes to write.

Ask→
- **How were the animals on the ark in a similar situation to the animals in the movie?**
- **How was the situation of the animals on the ark different from what we saw in the movie?**

Let kids each read what they've written. Encourage kids to try to make their voices sound like the animals' voices they're portraying.

THE TOWER OF BABEL

UNMASKED! • *Scripture: Genesis 11:1-8*

 Movie Title:
THE WIZARD OF OZ (G)

Start Time: 47 minutes, 37 seconds

Where to Begin: Dorothy and her friends approach the wizard near the end of the movie.

Where to End: The wizard admits he's a fake.

Plot: Dorothy and her friends unmask the Wizard for what he really is—a mere man.

Use this clip to teach children about God's omnipotence, spiritual gifts, or the perils of pride.

Review: You can use this scene to help children understand that God sees who they really are inside—and loves them just the same! The Wizard was trying to be something he could never be—a supernatural being. The builders of the Tower of Babel were trying to make a name for themselves without God, much as the Wizard had tried to build a reputation using curtains and a disguised voice. In the end, both were unmasked and brought down to size.

Supplies: Masking tape, and a balloon and marker for each child

Preshow: If you have mostly young children in class or a limited amount of time, inflate and tie off the balloons before class. Place the inflated balloons in a large trash bag.

now playing

Give each child a balloon. (If you didn't inflate and tie off the balloons before class, have kids do so now.)

Say→ Just as your balloons are puffed up with air, people sometimes get puffed up with pride. We're going to watch a scene from *The Wizard of Oz*. In this scene, Dorothy and her friends approach the Wizard. As you watch, write on your balloon words that describe what the Wizard is trying to make his visitors think of him. For example, you might write, "powerful" or "wise." Let's watch.

Show the clip from *The Wizard of Oz*.

Ask→ • What words did you write on your balloon?
• Did any of the words you wrote describe what the Wizard was *really* like? Explain.

Say→ The Wizard was trying to be something he wasn't. He was trying to act powerful, as if he had special powers. But he was just a man. He kind of reminds me of the people who built the Tower of Babel. They were trying to make a big name for themselves on their own, without remembering what God had done for them. Now on your balloon, write one word that describes what kids your age sometimes get puffed up with pride about.

After kids write, let them tape their balloons to a wall to build a "tower." Then explain that just as the Wizard was discovered for who he really was, the builders of the Tower of Babel were reminded by God that they weren't as powerful as they thought. Let kids pop the balloons. Then remind kids that God sees them for who they really are and loves them just as they are!

THE QUACK • *Scripture: Genesis 11:1-8*

Movie Title:
DOCTOR DOOLITTLE (1967) (nOT RATED)

Start Time: 2 minutes, 14 seconds

Where to Begin: Dr. Doolittle first demonstrates his ability to talk with the animals—in this case, a duck!

Where to End: He stops talking to the duck.

The Critics Say

Use this clip to help children understand that God is in control of the world. You could also teach about reliance on God or trusting God with our lives and plans.

Plot: Dr. Doolittle, an eccentric veterinarian who converses with animals, has just received two visitors, his friend Matthew and a young boy named Tommy Stubbins. Tommy has brought a duck with an injured wing, and is astounded to see Dr. Doolittle having a "conversation" with the duck.

Review: You can use this scene to help children understand that God is in control of the world and that he understands us completely. When those who were constructing the Tower of Babel thought they could build a tower that touched heaven, God stepped in and confused their languages so they couldn't understand each other. In this movie clip, Dr. Doolittle is the only person who can understand the animals. To everyone else, their language is incomprehensible. Use the confusion of languages as a springboard to encourage kids that God understands and is in control of *all* creation!

now PLAYING

Say→ We're going to watch a scene from *Doctor Doolittle.* The doctor is the only person in the movie who can understand what the animals are saying. To everyone else, the animals' language makes no sense. Let's watch.

Show the clip from *Doctor Doolittle.*

Ask→ • How do you think the animals felt before they discovered that Dr. Doolittle could understand them?
• How would you feel if hardly anyone understood what you said?

Say→ The people who built the Tower of Babel found out the hard way what it was like not to be understood. They thought they could build a tower to heaven, and they forgot all about God in the process. So God confused their languages so they couldn't understand each other. Let's see what that may have been like.

Have kids each make up a pretend language, the louder the better. Then tell children to go around the room and greet each of the other children in their new languages. After kids have all greeted one another, gather everyone together.

Ask→ • What was it like speaking in a language no one could understand?
• How would your life be different if no one could understand you?
• How do you think the animals in the movie felt when they realized the doctor could actually understand them?
• How does it make you feel to know that God always understands you, no matter what language you speak?

THE THREE VISITORS

WELCOME! • *Scripture: Genesis 18:1-15*

Movie Title:
OLD YELLER (NOT RATED)

Start Time: 36 minutes, 22 seconds

Where to Begin: A stranger, Old Yeller's real owner, generously makes a deal to allow Old Yeller to stay with the Coates' family.

The Critics Say

You could use this clip to teach children about hospitality, friendship, or sharing.

Where to End: Following a meal, the stranger leaves.

Plot: The Coates family, including Mrs. Coates, her two boys, and their "old yeller" dog, live in rural Texas just after the Civil War. Mr. Coates is away on a cattle drive to earn money for the family. One day a stranger comes to visit, and he is welcomed and given a good home-cooked meal.

Review: You can use this scene to help children identify with how the three visitors who arrived at Abraham's tent were treated. Although they were strangers, the three visitors were heartily welcomed. Abraham offered to wash their feet, gave them water, and oversaw the preparation of a special meal to feed his guests. In a world where strangers are often viewed as dangerous, this movie clip can help kids see a family, with children just like them, showing hospitality to a stranger. Just as in the Bible story, the stranger in the movie has a surprise identity (he's the owner of Old Yeller). Also similar to the Bible story where the three strangers brought welcome news, the stranger in the movie gave welcome news when he decided to leave the dog with the family, rather than claim him as his own.

Supplies: Construction paper, markers, and glitter glue

NOW PLAYING

Gather kids together.

Ask→ • When your family has company, what do you do to get ready for your visitors?

• What would your family do if company just showed up on your doorstep?

Say→ We're going to watch a scene from a movie called *Old Yeller*. It's about a family in Texas who take in a yellow dog. The story takes place just after the Civil War, and the father of the family is away when they receive unexpected company. Let's see what happens.

Show the *Old Yeller* clip.

Ask→ • How do you think the family felt when a strange man showed up at their ranch?

- Why do you think they showed the stranger such hospitality by inviting him in and taking care of him?

Say→ The family showed the stranger such hospitality because travelers in that time often had to ride their horses long distances between towns. A traveler would need to give water to his horse, rest, and eat before he could go on.

That's a lot like how Abraham treated his three visitors in the Bible. People in Bible times usually traveled by foot, so they would have been tired, thirsty, and hungry, too. In both the Bible story and the movie, the strangers were welcomed with great hospitality. Let's make welcome mats so we can greet visitors the same way.

Set out construction paper, markers, and glitter glue for kids to share. Let kids design their own welcome mats or signs to use at home. You could also make a larger class welcome mat or sign to use outside your classroom.

DO I KNOW YOU? • *Scripture: Genesis 18:1-15*

Movie Title:
THE PARENT TRAP (1961) (NOT RATED)

Start Time: 22 minutes, 13 seconds

Where to Begin: The first twin switches identities with her sister and goes unrecognized by her sister's family.

You could use this movie clip to teach children that God knows all about them and that he values what's in their hearts, rather than their outward appearance.

Where to End: The mother and daughter go upstairs.

Plot: Identical twins, separated since early childhood, are reunited at summer camp. They form a plan to switch places in their respective families in an attempt to get their parents back together.

Review: You can use this scene to introduce and highlight the fact that Abraham didn't recognize the real identity of the three visitors to his tent. In the movie clip, identical twins switch families in an attempt to reunite their parents. Their families don't recognize who they really are, just as Abraham didn't know who his three visitors really were.

Supplies: A table or chairs and a blanket

Preshow: Before class, set up a barrier for kids to hide behind by stretching a blanket over a table or two chairs.

NOW PLAYING

Say→ Today we're going to watch a scene from an old movie called *The Parent Trap*. Identical twins, who had been separated since they were little, meet again at summer camp. They decide to switch families and try to get their divorced parents back together. Let's see what happens when they switch families.

Show the clip from *The Parent Trap.*

Ask➜ • **How do you think the twins felt when they met their new families?**
• **Did you think the parents would be able to tell that the twins had switched places? Why or why not?**

Say➜ **The parents in the movie couldn't tell that they had the wrong twins because they didn't recognize which girl was which. They couldn't tell who the twins actually were. In the Bible story of the three visitors who went to see Abraham, Abraham couldn't tell who his guests really were either.**

Let's play a game to see what it might be like not to be able to recognize someone.

Choose a volunteer to briefly leave the room or close his or her eyes. Have everyone else hide behind the barrier you constructed before this activity. Then let your volunteer try to guess the identities of the children behind the barrier.

You can play this game in a variety of ways. Kids behind the barrier could disguise their voices, show only their hands or feet, or answer questions posed by the volunteer. Play several rounds as you choose new volunteers. After the game, have everyone sit with you behind the barrier.

Ask➜ • **What was it like to try to hide your real identity?**
• **What was it like to try to guess someone's identity?**
• **How is that like the movie clip we watched?**
• **How is that like the story of Abraham's three visitors?**

Say➜ **In our game, we had fun trying to guess each other's identities. But it's good to know that in real life, we don't have to worry about whether God really knows us or not. God knows us inside and out, and he knows what's in our hearts. And guess what else? God loves us, too!**

ABRAHAM IS TESTED

WHO DO YOU TRUST? • *Scripture: Genesis 22:1-18*

 Movie Title:
PETER PAN (1953) (NOT RATED)

Start Time: 1 hour, 2 minutes, 35 seconds

Where to Begin: The pirates are dancing a circle around the Lost Boys and Wendy who are tied up.

You can also use this clip to teach children about trust, friendship, or faithfulness.

Where to End: Captain Hook mocks Wendy as she says that Peter Pan will save them.

Plot: Captain Hook has captured the Lost Boys and orders them to become pirates or walk the plank. Wendy challenges them to hold fast and trust Peter Pan to help them.

Review: You can use this scene to help children understand that sometimes it's hard to trust God and we all need encouragement to do just that. The Lost Boys were scared and in a bad situation. Wendy reminded them that they could trust Peter Pan to help. Abraham trusted God, even when he could have run away from his bad situation.

Supplies: Chairs, tables, and other "obstacles" for children to get around

Preshow: Decide how much space you will use for your obstacle course and have the necessary obstacles available.

nOW PLAYING

Begin by allowing the kids to set up an obstacle course using chairs, tables, or other items. Show them the path they will follow to complete the obstacle course. Allow each child to complete the course at least once. You may change the course or the path children follow to allow them to take more turns.

Say→ **We're going to watch a scene from *Peter Pan*. Captain Hook has captured the Lost Boys and urges them to become pirates or face a penalty of "walking the plank." Wendy challenges them to stand strong and wait for Peter Pan to help. Let's watch.**

Show the *Peter Pan* clip.

Ask→ • **How do you think the Lost Boys felt when Captain Hook captured them?**
• **Why would it have been hard for the Lost Boys and Wendy to trust Peter Pan to help them?**

Say→ **God wants us to trust him with everything we have and in everything we do. Sometimes the things we own or the things we enjoy doing seem more important to us than trusting in God. We let an "obstacle course" get between us and God. Or maybe we get scared and we forget that we can trust God.**

Abraham trusted God with the life of his son Isaac. Abraham may have been scared or worried, but he knew that he could trust God even in a bad situation.

Ask→ • **In the video we just watched, why do you think Wendy may have trusted Peter Pan?**
• **Why can we trust God?**

DECISIONS, DECISIONS • *Scripture: Genesis 22:1-18*

Movie Title:
ALADDIN (G)

Start Time: 1 hour, 22 minutes, 16 seconds

Where to Begin: Aladdin apologizes to Princess Jasmine for lying about being a prince.

You can also use this clip to teach children about making good choices, kindness, or keeping promises.

The Critics Say

Where to End: Aladdin wishes for "the Nile," and the Genie says, "No way!"

Plot: Aladdin sacrifices his final wish to set the Genie free, while the Genie is willing to sacrifice his freedom to help Aladdin be a prince again.

Review: You can use this scene to help children learn about making good decisions. Aladdin had to decide whether to keep his promise or break it to help himself. Abraham made a good decision because he trusted God. We all need to learn to make good decisions and that starts with doing God's will!

Supplies: Ten sheets of paper and a marker or pen

Preshow: Number four sheets of paper one to four. With the remaining six sheets of paper, place a large X on the left side and a large O on the right side of each sheet. Read and be sure you understand the Pyramid Choices game described below.

now playing

Say→ We're going to watch a scene from *Aladdin*. Aladdin is down to his last wish and must decide between keeping his promise to set the Genie free or using the wish to help himself become a prince. Let's watch.

Show the *Aladdin* clip.

Ask→ • How hard do you think it was for Aladdin to keep his promise?
• How do you think the Genie felt?

Say→ We're going to play Pyramid Choices, a decision-making game in which one decision causes you to follow a certain path.

In this activity, each child will choose either an X or O, and follow a path through the pyramid by following that letter.

Set up an inverted pyramid using the ten pieces of paper. Lay out the four numbered sheets in a row beside each other. Directly below that, form a second row using three of the X/O sheets so that they are staggered between the sheets in the first row. In the third row place two of the X/O sheets staggered between those in the second row. Place the final X/O sheet at the tip of the pyramid.

To play the game, have a child start in front of the first sheet of paper and turn away from the pyramid. For each child, randomly turn the X/O sheets so that some read O/X. Turning a few of the X/O papers around for each child will be enough to make each turn different. The child will then, without looking, choose either to follow the X path or the O path. Children will move to the right or left up to the next level based on which side of the

| 1 | 2 | 3 | 4 |

| XO | OX | OX |

| XO | XO |

| XO |

paper their letter is on. For example, if a child chooses to follow the X's and the X is on the left side of the paper, the child will move to the left as he or she goes to the next level. If neither side matches the child's choice, have the child continue in the direction of his or her last choice. At each paper the child will follow his or her letter to the next level until he or she arrives at a numbered paper. Players will stay on that number until another child lands on the same number. Then the first child will go to the end of the line for another turn as time allows.

Ask→ • **How is this activity similar to the choices we make in real life?**

Say→ **When we make choices they will affect our future choices as well. Abraham made a choice to trust God. That choice led him up a mountain where he could have lost his son. But Abraham made a good choice by trusting God. God protected Isaac and blessed Abraham for making the right choice.**

Ask→ • **How can we learn to make good choices?**

ISAAC'S BLESSING

ME FIRST • *Scripture: Genesis 27:1-40*

Movie Title:

🎥 **THE ARISTOCATS (G)**

You can also use this clip to teach children about greed, envy, or handling disappointment.

The Critics Say

Start Time: 7 minutes, 45 seconds

Where to Begin: The lawyer is dancing toward the desk and says, "Splendid, splendid. Who do you want me to sue?"

Where to End: Edgar sees dollar signs and says, "Those cats have got to go."

Plot: Edgar (the butler) gets greedy when he overhears his eccentric boss's plans to give her estate to her cats ahead of him. Edgar begins to think about how to get the cats out of the way.

Review: You can use this clip to help children understand how envy and greed can cause problems for us. Edgar got greedy, wanting things for himself. This caused him to get increasingly upset and to plot about how to get the money for himself. He did things that were wrong so he could get his own way. Jacob wanted his father's blessing so much that he treated his brother and his father poorly to get it. But God wants us to do what is right. He wants us to do things his way not our own way.

NOW PLAYING

Start by playing Follow the Leader with a twist. There will be several "leaders" at the same time doing their own thing. Form three equal-sized groups, and assign a number to each group. Have each group take a turn being the leader. When a new number is called out (one, two, or three), everyone should try their best to follow and act out what the different leaders do. Give each group a couple of chances to be the leader. Allow for some confusion, and encourage the children to do the best they can at following the leaders.

Ask→ • **What was hard about playing Follow the Leader this way?**
• **How could having so many people who want to be first cause problems at school? at home? with your friends?**

Say→ We're going to watch a scene from *The Aristocats.* The butler, whose name is Edgar, hears his boss talking about who she will give her money and all of her stuff to. Edgar is surprised to hear that she wants to give it to her cats first. Let's watch.

Show *The Aristocats* clip.

Ask→ • **Why do you think Edgar was upset by his boss's choice to give her money to her cats first?**
• **How do you think he felt before he overheard his boss? after?**

Say→ Edgar got greedy when he heard that he was going to get money only after the cats. He wanted to be first! He was upset and disappointed. He didn't handle it too well.

God wants us to do what is right, even when we don't get our way. Jacob wanted the blessing from Isaac, his father. The blessing should have been for Esau, who was Jacob's older brother. Jacob, with the help of his mother, tricked Isaac into giving the blessing to him. Jacob took what belonged to his older brother. This caused problems between Jacob and Esau for years to come.

Ask→ • **How would you feel about playing with someone who wanted his or her own way all the time?**
• **What kind of problems may we run into if we do things that are wrong to help us get our own way?**

I'LL TAKE THAT • *Scripture: Genesis 27:1-40*

Movie Title:
TOY STORY 2 (G)

Start Time: 18 minutes, 6 seconds

Where to Begin: Woody is lying on the ground as a little girl picks him up.

You can also use this clip to teach children about respecting others, stealing, or greed.

Where to End: Al drives away, and a feather floats down in front of Buzz.

Plot: Al, the greedy collector and toy store owner, steals Woody from a yard sale after the mother tells him that the doll is not for sale.

Review: Al was more concerned about what he wanted than the fact that the doll belonged to someone else. This is similar to the way Jacob acted when he took his father's blessing that was intended for Esau.

Supplies: A personal item such as a coin, a toy, a set of keys, a Bible, or some other unbreakable item

Preshow: Gather a few small items in case children do not have personal items suitable for the activity.

now playing

Ask children each to choose one small, personal item that they can use in a game. You may suggest items like coins, toys, keys, Bibles, or other unbreakable items. Items within the room may also be used. Have children stand with their items and form a circle. For larger groups, form circles with no more than ten children in each.

Ask one child in the circle to take an object from any other person in the circle. That child will then sit down. The person whose object was taken will then take an object from another person who is standing. Continue this process until no one is left standing.

Repeat the game as time allows. Then have children retrieve their original items.

Say→ We're going to watch a scene from *Toy Story 2*. One of the toys, Woody, has accidentally been set out at a yard sale. Al, a greedy toy collector, sees Woody and wants to buy him. The mother refuses, but Al is determined to get his way. Let's watch.

Show the *Toy Story 2* clip.

Ask→ • Why did Al take Woody even after the mom told him he couldn't?
• How would you have felt if your toy was taken?

Say→ Taking something that is not ours is wrong, and it hurts the person we take it from. It also hurts us and can get us into a lot of trouble. Jacob took something that was not his. This caused problems for him and his family.

We can avoid many problems by considering others before ourselves and showing them respect. We can show respect for God and each other by how we treat other people and the things that belong to them.

The Critics Say

As a closing activity, you can change the activity from "taking" to "giving." Play will continue in the same manner, beginning with one child who "gives" his or her object away and then sits down.

JOSEPH IS SOLD BY HIS BROTHERS

MINE, ALL MINE • Scripture: Genesis 37:1-36

Movie Title:
CINDERELLA (1950) (NOT RATED)

You can also use this clip to teach the children about jealousy, favoritism, kindness, or sharing.

Start Time: 40 minutes, 52 seconds

Where to Begin: Cinderella yells, "Wait! Please wait for me!" as she comes down the steps in her new dress.

Where to End: Cinderella runs out of the house and collapses on a bench.

Plot: Cinderella's jealous stepsisters take back their discarded items from the dress that Cinderella was planning on wearing to the ball. The stepmother takes her daughters and leaves Cinderella in a mess.

Review: You can use this scene to help children understand that we need to be considerate of other people and their feelings. Cinderella was in a situation where her feelings were not considered. Jealousy can cause us to look at people in a negative way, just as Cinderella's stepmother and stepsisters looked at her. The same thing happened to Joseph when his brothers became jealous of him. They showed no concern for Joseph or for God who wants us to love each other.

NOW PLAYING

Have children form pairs. An adult can stand in if there are an uneven number of children. Have partners stand facing each other. Instruct the children to remember as much about how the other person looks as possible. After about thirty seconds, have the pairs stand back to back so they can no longer see each other. Instruct the children to raise their hands if the following statements are true about their partners. You can allow them to turn and face each other after each question to check their answers. Then have them turn back to back again.

Say→ I want you to think about your partner. If the following statements are true about your partner raise your hand.
- Your partner is wearing glasses.
- Your partner is wearing white shoes.
- Your partner is wearing a shirt with buttons.
- Your partner is wearing blue jeans.

You may add other statements of your own if you like.

Say→ We're going to watch a scene from *Cinderella*. Cinderella is wearing a dress made from the scraps of material left over from her stepsisters. The stepsisters are jealous. They think only of themselves and don't care about how Cinderella feels. Let's watch.

Show the *Cinderella* clip.

Ask→ • How do you think Cinderella felt?

Say→ Joseph may have felt as Cinderella did. Joseph's older brothers didn't like Joseph or the attention that he got from their father. When Joseph's brothers sold him into slavery, they showed that they were not concerned about Joseph or their father. Joseph's brothers were only worried about themselves.

God wants us to think about others and to treat them kindly. Jealousy can keep us thinking about ourselves and what we want. We can overcome these bad feelings with God's help. We can be considerate of other people and their feelings by focusing on them. More than just how they look, we can focus on how they may be feeling.

Ask→ • How can we show others that we care about them?

GREEN-EYED • Scripture: Genesis 37:1-36

Movie Title:
TOY STORY (G)

You can also use this clip to teach children about jealousy or anger.

Start Time: 37 minutes

Where to Begin: Andy needs to decide which toy to take to Pizza Planet.

Where to End: The other toys accuse Woody of pushing Buzz out of the window. They are just about to capture him when they hear Andy coming to his room, looking for Buzz.

Plot: Woody has been Andy's favorite toy for many years. When Andy receives a Buzz Lightyear toy for his birthday, Andy's attention diverts to Buzz. Woody becomes jealous of Buzz. He takes his anger out on Buzz by causing an accident. Though Woody intends to only push Buzz behind a dresser, Woody accidentally causes Buzz to fall out of the two-story window.

Review: You can use this scene to help children understand how Joseph's brothers felt about Joseph. Because Joseph was his father's favored son, Joseph's brothers were jealous of him and plotted to kill him. Jealousy is often accompanied with anger, hatred, and bitterness. We can ask God to help us overcome the sin of jealousy.

Supplies: Gingerbread-man cookies (store-bought is fine), pressed fruit rolls, plastic knives, and paper plates

Preshow: Place two cookies and a plastic knife on each child's plate. Place fruit rolls in the center of the table to share.

now playing

Say→ We're going to watch a scene from *Toy Story*. Woody is jealous of Buzz Lightyear, Andy's new toy. Woody had always been Andy's favorite, until Andy received Buzz from his mom on his birthday. Let's watch to see what the sin of jealousy causes Woody to do.

Show the *Toy Story* clip.

Ask→ • How did Woody feel about all the attention Buzz was getting?
• How did Woody feel after Buzz fell out of the window?

Say→ Did you know that the Bible tells us that jealousy is a sin? Not only is jealousy a sin, but jealousy often leads to other sins. Let's hear a story about a time in the Bible when jealousy caused a family of brothers to commit other sins.

Summarize or read Genesis 37:1-36.

Say→ Join me at the table, and let's use these cookies to retell the story about Joseph and his brothers.

Have the children find a place at the table. Ask them to use the plastic knives to cut small strips of fruit roll to put around one of the cookies to make a many-colored coat like the one Joseph had. Tell the children to hold one cookie in each hand.

Say→ Look at your two cookies.

Ask→ • How are the two cookies different?

Say→ Joseph's brothers were jealous because their father favored Joseph and gave him a nice coat. I'm sure the brothers had coats, too, but maybe they thought Joseph's coat was a lot nicer.

Jealousy is a sin. Jealousy causes other sins such as anger, hatred, unkind words, and bitterness. Jealousy causes us to do bad things, just like when Woody pushed Buzz and when Joseph's brothers sold him into slavery.

God does not want us to be jealous. We can ask God to help us overcome our jealousy.

Ask→ • How is what Woody did to Buzz kind of like what Joseph's brothers did to Joseph?
• How is it different?
• What can you do when you feel jealous?

JOSEPH MAKES HIMSELF KNOWN

BAD INTO GOOD • *Scripture: Genesis 45:1-28; 50:19-21*

Movie Title:
JOSEPH, KING OF DREAMS (NOT RATED)

Start Time: 1 hour, 11 minutes, 48 seconds

> The Critics Say
>
> You can also use this clip to teach children about forgiveness, obeying God, and God's plan for us.

Where to Begin: Joseph accuses his brothers of taking the cup.

Where to End: Joseph tells his brothers that they, their families, and their father will come to live with him in Egypt.

Plot: Joseph threatens to put Benjamin in prison for stealing a gold cup. Each brother begs for Joseph to put him in prison instead of Benjamin. They confess that they hurt their father by selling Joseph many years ago and beg to be punished instead. Joseph announces that he is their brother and forgave them a long time ago. He tells them to come live with him in Egypt so that they can be fed and taken care of.

Review: You can use this scene to help children understand that God can work good through bad situations. Even though Joseph's brothers sold him into slavery, God worked good things out of this bad situation. God allowed Joseph to find favor with his master and eventually to be put in charge of Egypt by Pharaoh. This allowed Joseph to help his family and many others during the famine.

Supplies: Cereal, large containers, one-cup measuring cups, and quart-sized resealable bags

Preshow: Pour cereal into one large container for every four or five children. Put a measuring cup into each container.

NOW PLAYING

Say→ We're going to watch a scene from *Joseph, King of Dreams.* Joseph's brothers had sold him many years before this scene. There was a great famine in the land, which means there was very little food. When the brothers went to Egypt to try to get food, Joseph was there. The brothers did not even recognize him. Let's watch and see what happens.

Show the *Joseph, King of Dreams* clip.

Ask→ • How do you think Joseph felt when he saw his brothers?
• How do you think Joseph's brothers felt when they recognized Joseph?

Say→ God did not promise us that everything that happens to us will be good. But God does promise to be with us, in good times and in bad times. In bad situations, God can make good things happen. Even though Joseph's brothers sold him into slavery, God used that situation for good. In time, the Pharaoh of Egypt put Joseph in charge of Egypt. Because of this job, Joseph helped all of his family and many other people during the great famine.

Let's play a game to remind us that God worked good through Joseph's bad times.

Have children form groups of four or five. Choose one person in each team to be "Joseph." Give each Joseph a container of cereal. Give the remaining team players a resealable bag. Those players will be "Joseph's brothers." Have all of the Josephs stand at one end of the room and Joseph's brothers at the other end of the room. Have each Joseph scoop a cup of cereal from the container and race to a brother, pouring the cereal into his or her bag. Joseph should return to the container to scoop and pour cereal until each teammate's bag has cereal. Continue playing until each person has a turn being Joseph.

Say→ God worked good through Joseph's bad situation. God can work good through our bad times, too.

Ask→ • Can you tell me about a time when something bad happened to you and God worked good through that bad time?
• What can we do when bad things happen to us?
• How can we help others when bad things happen to them?

TOTALLY FORGIVEN • *Scripture: Genesis 45:1-28; 50:19-21*

 *Movie Title:*
TARZAN (ANIMATED DISNEY VERSION) (G)

You can also use this clip to teach children about honoring our parents.

The Critics Say

Start Time: 1 hour, 27 minutes, 55 seconds

Where to Begin: Tarzan comforts an injured Kerchak and asks for his forgiveness.

Where to End: Tarzan, the new leader of the gorilla family, walks away with the gorillas following him.

Plot: After Tarzan's parents were killed by a cheetah, the infant boy is raised by a pack of gorillas. Tarzan struggles for acceptance and always feels out of place. The leading silverback, Kerchak, doesn't accept Tarzan until moments before he dies after being shot by a hunter.

Review: You can use this scene to help children understand the concept of forgiveness. Just as Joseph forgave his brothers for selling him into slavery, Tarzan and Kerchak forgave one another for their wrongdoings. This will help children understand our need to forgive others as God has forgiven us. Because God forgives us, we are able to forgive others.

Supplies: A pen and paper

Preshow: Write the suggested story scenes (or make up your own) on separate pieces of paper.

The Critics Say

A fight between Tarzan and a poacher occurs just before this suggested scene. Be sure to have the movie at the exact spot so as not to frighten younger children with the fight scene.

now PLAYING

Say→ We're going to watch a scene from *Tarzan.* Tarzan is sad that he caused his gorilla family to be hurt by bringing humans into their village. Let's listen to what Tarzan says to his gorilla father, Kerchak, and how Kerchak responds.

Show the *Tarzan* clip.

Ask→ • How did Tarzan feel about what happened to Kerchak?
• What did Tarzan say to Kerchak?
• Did Kerchak forgive Tarzan?

Say→ Tarzan felt badly about causing harm to his gorilla family. He asked forgiveness from Kerchak, his gorilla father. Kerchak forgave Tarzan. Kerchak asked Tarzan's forgiveness, and Tarzan forgave Kerchak.

When we wrong someone, we should ask that person's forgiveness. And in turn, when someone wrongs us and asks for forgiveness, we should forgive them. Let's listen to our story about Joseph and see how he forgives his brothers.

Read or summarize Genesis 45:1-28; 50:19-21.

Say→ Joseph forgave his brothers. With God's help, we can forgive others also. God teaches us to forgive others by his example of always forgiving our sins.

Let's act out times in our lives when we need to forgive others.

Form pairs. Give each pair a scene to act out, and select a character for each child. Let one pair at a time pantomime the scene using words and actions. Encourage children to end each scene with a display of forgiveness. After each scene, ask the questions below. Do as many scenes as time allows.

Scene 1: Your friend borrowed your favorite book and lost it.

Scene 2: Your sister took one of your toys without asking.

Scene 3: Your brother called you a crybaby when you stubbed your toe and cried.

Scene 4: Your friend said she wouldn't be your friend anymore unless she got to be first on the swing.

Ask→ • What wrongdoing took place in this scene?
• How did our characters make the situation right?
• What do you do when you have wronged a friend?

THE BIRTH OF MOSES

LETTING GO TO FOLLOW GOD • *Scripture: Exodus 2:1-8*

Movie Title:
THE FOX AND THE HOUND (G)

Start Time: 52 minutes, 28 seconds

Where to Begin: The older woman decides she must take Tod to the forest.

> *The Critics Say*
> You can also use this clip to teach children about selflessness, difficulties, and obeying God.

Where to End: The older woman leaves Tod in the woods and drives away.

Plot: Tod, a baby fox lives with an older woman. Tod befriends a neighbor's hunting pup, which eventually causes the grouchy neighbor to believe Tod is a nuisance and chicken chaser. The older woman, even though she dearly loves her pet, knows she must release him back into the wild for his own safety.

Review: You can use this scene to help children understand how Moses' mother must have felt when she placed Moses in the basket in the river. Though she dearly loved Moses, she knew she had to let him go for his safety and as part of God's plan. Sometimes we have to let go of things we love in order to follow God's plan.

Supplies: A laundry basket, drawing paper, markers or crayons, scissors, rope, and blue bulletin board paper

Preshow: Stretch out a long sheet of blue bulletin board paper on the floor, to resemble a river. Tie one end of a rope to the basket, and place it at the beginning of the "river."

NOW PLAYING

Place scissors, markers or crayons and drawing paper on a table. Have each child draw an outline of a child and color it to resemble his or her best friend. Have children cut out the outlines and hold onto the pictures.

Say→ We're going to watch a scene from *The Fox and the Hound*. Tod, a pet fox, is living with an older woman. The fox likes to play with the neighbor's hunting dog. But the grouchy, hunting neighbor doesn't like Tod and thinks he's a pest. He blames the fox for the injury his other dog had and for chasing his chickens. The older woman realizes Tod is not safe as long as he is living next to the hunter. Let's watch to see what the lady does with the fox.

Show the clip from *The Fox and the Hound*.

Ask→ • How did the woman feel about taking Tod back to the woods?
• Why do you think she took him to the woods?

Say→ Even though the woman loved Tod very much, she knew she must release him. She knew that was best for him. That's just like our story about Moses. Even though Moses' mom loved Moses very much, she knew that she had to let him go to save him.

In our lives, we may have to let go of something that we love, as part of God's plan.

Ask→ • Has there ever been a time in your life that you had to let go of something you loved?

Say→ Raise your hand if you've ever had to move. God sometimes has plans for us to move to a new home or even a new state. When we move, we have to leave our friends behind. We have to give up friends we love as part of God's plan. Let's pretend that you have just found out that you're going to move far away from your best friend. You're very sad to lose your friend, but you know that it's part of God's plan for you to move. Let's place our outlines of our friends in this basket, just as Moses' mom placed him in a basket.

After everyone has placed their pictures in the basket, use the rope to pull the basket along the "river," away from the kids. Have the children wave and say goodbye.

Ask→ • How did you feel about having to say goodbye to your friends?
• How is that like the way Moses' mom felt when she put Moses in the basket on the river?
• How is it different?

Allow children to go get their pictures.

GOD HAS PLANS • *Scripture: Exodus 2:1-8*

Movie Title:
THE PRINCE OF EGYPT (PG)

The Critics Say

You can use this clip to teach children that God's plans are best. You can also use it to teach about difficulties.

Start Time: 8 minutes, 7 seconds

Where to Begin: Moses' mother places Moses in the basket in the river.

Where to End: Moses' sister sees that Moses is rescued and safe.

Plot: In order to protect baby Moses from being killed, his mother places him in a basket and puts the basket in the river. He is found by an Egyptian woman who raises the baby as her own. Eventually, Moses grows up to be the man who leads God's people out of bondage in Egypt.

Review: You can use this scene to help children understand that God has good plans for us. As a baby boy in Pharaoh's time, Moses seemed destined to death. But God had good plans for his life. Moses was rescued by Pharaoh's family and raised in Egypt, which was all a part of God's preparation of Moses to be the leader of God's people. God has good plans for each one of us, too. And God will make provisions to see that those plans are carried out.

Supplies: Sponges, scissors, small wooden ice-cream spoons, markers, and tissues

Preshow: Cut each sponge in half, forming two squares.

NOW PLAYING

Say→ We're going to watch a scene from *The Prince of Egypt*. Pharaoh was worried that the Israelites would outnumber the Egyptians. He decided to get rid of all the baby boys. Things did not look good for baby Moses. Let's watch to see what happens to baby Moses.

Show the clip from *The Prince of Egypt*.

Ask→ • How do you think Moses' mother felt when she sent her baby in a basket down the river?

• How do you think Moses' sister felt when she saw that Moses was rescued and safe?

Say→ God had good plans for Moses. He kept him safe and gave him an Egyptian home to grow up in so that he would not be killed as a baby. God has good plans for us, too. God will make sure his good plans for us are carried out. Let's make a take-home basket to remind us that God has good plans for us, just as he did for Moses.

Give each child a sponge square. Then have each child draw a face on the wooden spoon and wrap it in a tissue. Show the child how to lay "baby Moses" on the sponge "basket."

Say→ Take your Moses' basket home and place it in your room. It can be a constant reminder that God has good plans for you. You can also float your Moses basket in the tub to remind you of today's story. Just remember to let it dry before you take it back to your room!

Ask→ • How did God provide for Moses in order for God's plans to take place?

• How can you know of God's plans for you?

• Whom can you tell the story of Moses?

MOSES AND THE BURNING BUSH

MISSION POSSIBLE • Scripture: Exodus 3:1-7

 Movie Title:
A BUG'S LIFE (G)

Start Time: 24 minutes, 55 seconds

Where to Begin: Hopper demands to know where his food is.

Where to End: Hopper says, "Someone can get hurt."

You can use this clip to teach children about bullying, God's care for us in difficult times, and God's love for us.

The Critics Say

Plot: The grasshoppers visit the ants to get the food they have extorted, just as they have done every year. Hopper, the leader of the grasshoppers discovers that the ants do not have the food ready and demands they get it ready right away.

Review: The plight of the ant colony is similar to the years of oppression the Hebrew slaves experienced in Egypt. You can use this clip to help the children empathize with the enslaved ants' fear and frustration. Once this emotional connection is built, it's a small jump to understanding the state of the Hebrews and how their loving God ached for their freedom.

Preshow: Secure a wide-open space at your church where your children can play a tag game.

Little children may find this scene frightening. If you have young children in your class, you might not want to show it.

now PLAYING

Take the class to a place where the children have room to run.

Say→ Let's play Chore Tag. One person is "It." If "It" tags you, "It" will tell you a chore that you have to pretend to do. You have to pretend to do that chore for "It." I will choose another person to be the "Rescuer." The Rescuer's job is to tag anyone who is doing chores. If the Rescuer taps you on the head you are free.

Play several rounds of the game. Switch roles often to allow as many children as possible to have a turn.

If space is tight, have the children "run" on their knees or "heel-to-toe."

Ask→ • How did it feel to be stuck doing chores?
• What was it like being the Rescuer?
• How would you feel if a stranger made you do his or her chores?

Say→ We are about to view a scene from *A Bug's Life*. The ants are slaves to the grasshoppers. The grasshoppers make the ants collect food for them every year. The ants had an accident and lost the food they were to give the grasshoppers. Watch how Hopper, the leader of the grasshoppers responds.

Show the *Bug's Life* clip.

Ask→ • Do you think the grasshoppers were treating the ants fairly?
• How would you feel if you were an ant that lived in the colony?
• How would you feel if your best friend was someone's slave? What would you do?

Say→ There was a time when God's special people were slaves to the Egyptians. God didn't want his people to suffer. Let's read what God did. Read Exodus 3:1-7.

Ask→ • Why do you think God cared about the Hebrew slaves?
• How do you think Moses felt after God told him that he cared about the hard times of his people? Why?

Say→ God cares for us when we are going through hard times, too.

Movie Title:

THE HOBBIT (ABC VIDEO, 1977) (NOT RATED)

The Critics Say

You can also use this clip to teach children about courage or God's calling.

Start Time: 4 minutes, 39 seconds

Where to Begin: Thorin says, "I assume the adventure is known to all."

Where to End: Gandalf says, "And so we begin our adventure."

Plot: Bilbo Baggins' peaceful existence is interrupted by a band of dwarfs and the wizard Gandalf. They bull into Bilbo's home and have a feast. Bilbo realizes that they are recruiting him for a dangerous adventure, and Bilbo becomes frightened.

Review: You can use this clip to help children understand that when God gives them a big job to do, it's OK to be scared. Like Bilbo, Moses needed to be confronted with his serene life. We can teach our children that God challenges each of them with a mission and purpose for their lives.

The Critics Say

The Hobbit was written by J.R.R. Tolkien. Tolkien was a devout Catholic and is credited with being at least partially responsible for leading C.S. Lewis to Christ. However, Tolkien used magic and wizardry as a literary device throughout his books on Middle Earth. If you feel the families in your ministry may object to this, you probably shouldn't show this clip.

Supplies: Sticky notes

NOW PLAYING

Gather the class along a wall. Give each child five sticky notes.

Say➔ **These sticky notes make up your "fear-o-meter." I will give you a situation. If you think that the situation is not scary at all place one sticky note on the wall. If you think the situation is very scary, place all of the sticky notes on the wall. If you think the situation is somewhere in between, you can place a few sticky notes on the wall. Ready?**

Call out scary and not so scary situations like "A strange dog growls at you," "Mom is serving brussel sprouts," or "It's thundering all night." Let the children call out scary situations, and have everyone measure it on their fear-o-meters. After each situation, have the children collect their sticky notes.

Say➔ **We're going to watch a movie clip from *The Hobbit*. Bilbo is minding his own business when a strange group shows up and tries to get him to join their dangerous adventure. Pay close attention to the way Bilbo feels.**

Play the *Hobbit* clip.

Say→ Rate how scared Bilbo felt with your fear-o-meters. Pause. **Now rate how you would have felt if you were in Bilbo's shoes.**

This reminds me of a time when God called Moses to join him on a special and dangerous mission. Moses was taking care of sheep when he saw a bush that had fire coming out of it, but the bush was not burning up! Moses approached the bush, and God talked to Moses from the bush. God told Moses that he chose him for a great adventure. Moses was to free God's people from the evil Pharaoh. Moses' family and friends were slaves in Egypt. Pharaoh had great armies. It would be a very dangerous job.

Use your fear-o-meters to rate how you think Moses felt.

Ask→ • **Why did you choose that rating?**
• **Has God ever asked you to do something that seemed scary for you to do?**
• **How is this story like the story in the movie clip?**
• **How is it different?**

Say→ **God promised to help Moses in his adventure. Moses was terrified, but he obeyed God and rescued his people from Pharaoh. We can trust God and obey him even when we are afraid of the consequences.**

THE PLAGUES

LET MY PEOPLE BE! • *Scripture: Exodus 7:14–11:10*

Movie Title:
THE IRON GIANT

You can also use this clip to teach children about God's might or handling "impossible" situations.

Start Time: 1 hour, 14 minutes

Where to Begin: The Iron Giant looks at his injured friend and gasps.

Where to End: The general says, "We can't stop this thing. We've hit it with everything we have."

Plot: The army mistakenly thinks that the Iron Giant is dangerous and has set out to destroy it. But the Iron Giant is actually peaceful, in spite of his intimidating power. He tries to evade the armies until his boy companion, Hogart, is injured while fleeing. The Iron Giant sets aside his peaceful ways and defends his helpless friend with awesome power.

Review: You can use this scene to explain to children that God was willing to use his awesome power to coerce the evil Pharaoh into freeing the Hebrew people from their slavery. God is fiercely loyal to his children. We can instill confidence in our children with the knowledge that God is for them!

Supplies: Balloons, brooms, and masking tape

Preshow: Divide the room in half with a masking tape line. Clear the playing area of any obstacles.

NOW PLAYING

Divide the class into two teams. Direct teams to opposite sides of the tape line. Give each child a broom.

The Critics Say: This clip is not suitable for younger children due to the intense transformation of the Iron Giant from a lovable friend into a fierce fighting machine. Teachers of young children should consider using "God Sticks Up for Us" (see below).

Say→ We're going to play a game in which you need to defend your side of the room from the balloons. If a balloon comes on your side of the room, brush it to the other side with your broom. Drop several balloons in the center of the room. After several moments, stop the game.

Ask→ • What was it like to defend your side of the room against attack?
• How did you feel when people tried to fill your half of the room with balloons?

Say→ We're going to watch a movie clip from *The Iron Giant*. The Iron Giant is a big, gentle robot who made friends with a boy named Hogart. The Giant really is gentle, but watch what happens when he needs to protect Hobart!

The Critics Say: Need more brooms? Before the lesson, mail a postcard to each of the children asking them to bring in a few.

Play the *Iron Giant* clip.

Say→ The Iron Giant really showed his power to protect his friend. This reminds me of what God did for his people. The Israelites were slaves to the Egyptians. God sent Moses to Egypt to warn Pharaoh to let his people go. Pharaoh would not listen, so God used his mighty power to convince Pharaoh to change his mind. God sent frogs, insects, hail, boils, and many other nasty things to Egypt to make Pharaoh change his mind. God is loving, but he will stick up for his loved ones. Isn't it good to know that you are all loved by God!

Ask→ • How is the movie clip similar to what God did to the Egyptians?
• How is it different?
• What is the best part of knowing that God sticks up for his children?
• How can knowing that give you courage at school? on the playground? when you're scared?

GOD STICKS UP FOR US • Scripture: Exodus 7:14–11:10

Movie Title:
THE JUNGLE BOOK (ANIMATED, 1967) (NOT RATED)

Start Time: 14 minutes, 10 seconds

Where to Begin: Kaa, the snake, says, "What have we here?"

Where to End: Mowgli says, "Kaa has a knot in his tail!"

Plot: The cunning boa constrictor, Kaa, has Mowgli hypnotized. While Mowgli is in a stupor, Kaa wraps him up in his coils. Bagheera hears the commotion and comes to the rescue.

You can also use this clip to teach about loyalty to friends.

The Critics Say

Review: You can use this clip to help children understand that God sticks up for his children. Kaa is like the Pharaoh, who had the children of Israel locked in his clutches. When God unleashed his plagues, it was similar to the way Bagheera fought on Mowgli's behalf. We are all like Mowgli. We are powerless to break the cords of our sin. We can teach children that Jesus sticks up for us and protects us from harm.

Supplies: Balloons, string, scissors, poster board, and a marker

Preshow: For each child cut a three-foot length of string. Inflate and tie a balloon for each child. Tie one end of each piece of string to a balloon.

NOW PLAYING

Give each child a balloon. Have children tie the free end of the string around their ankles.

Say→ We're going to play a game. The goal is to try to protect your balloon from everyone else. Stomp on the others' balloons. If your balloon is popped, you can still play and pop other people's balloons. Remember the goal is to keep your balloon safe.

Let the children play until all the balloons are popped.

Ask→ • What was it like trying to keep your balloon safe?
• What strategy did you use to protect your balloon?

Say→ Let's watch a clip from *The Jungle Book*. Bagheera, the panther, has agreed to deliver Mowgli to the man village. While Bagheera and Mowgli are asleep, Kaa, the evil snake, wants to eat Mowgli. Watch what happens.

Show the *Jungle Book* clip.

Ask→ • How was what Bagheera did like how you tried to protect your balloon?
• How do you think Mowgli felt knowing he had a friend like Bagheera?

If the children do not mention it, point out that unlike Bagheera, God is all-powerful. Bagheera needed some help for Mowgli. God does not need anyone's help in fighting his enemies.

The Critics Say

Say→ In the book of Exodus, there is a story about how the Egyptians had enslaved God's special people. Moses warned Pharaoh to let the people go free or bad things would happen to the Egyptians. Pharaoh would not let the people go, so God sent plagues on the Egyptians until Pharaoh let his people go.

Ask→ • **How is what Bagheera did for Mowgli like what God did for his people?**
- **How is it different?**
- **How does it feel knowing that God sticks up for his children?**

CROSSING THE RED SEA

DEAD END? • *Scripture: Exodus 13:17–14:31*

 *Movie Title:*
DINOSAUR (PG)

Start Time: 1 hour, 6 minutes

Where to Begin: The group of dinosaurs begins to play a game of I Spy.

Where to End: Aladar says, "We are not meant to survive."

> **The Critics Say**
> You can also use this clip to teach about discouragement. If you extend the clip for another minute, you can use this clip to discuss teamwork.

Plot: A pack of misfit dinosaurs is looking for an oasis of food and water after a meteor storm destroyed their feeding grounds. After overcoming many obstacles, the group is close to their destination. But they encounter a wall of boulders blocking their path and quickly become discouraged.

Review: You can use this clip to help children understand how the Hebrews felt when Moses led them out of Egypt only to encounter what appeared to be a dead end—the Red Sea. Aladar had led them to this point only to be thwarted by an obstacle he had no power to overcome. The clip captures the frustration of both the leader Aladar and his followers. Moses and his people must have felt misled by God as the enemy chariots advanced. However, God's direction was correct—even when it did not appear that way. We can use this story to teach children to have confidence in God's leading.

Supplies: Paper plate, cotton balls, glue, a paint stirrer, packing tape, and snacks

Preshow: Make a "cloud" by liberally fastening cotton balls to one side of a paper plate with glue. Fasten one end of a paint stirrer to the opposite side of the paper plate using the packing tape. Before class, hide the snacks in the same room as the TV/VCR.

NOW PLAYING

Say→ Let's play Follow the Cloud. Hold up the cloud. **If you follow this cloud, it will lead to some yummy snacks.** Lead the children through the church halls, then eventually back to the classroom.

Here we are. Go get your snack. Allow the children to question you concerning the snacks. **This reminds me of a movie I saw called *Dinosaur*. A**

dinosaur named Aladar was leading his friends to food and water. Dangerous Canotaurs were not far behind them. Let's see what happens.

Play the *Dinosaur* clip.

Ask→
- How did the dinosaurs feel when their path was blocked by the wall of boulders?
- Why do you think Aladar was so discouraged?

Say→ Aladar was the leader. When he realized that he led the dinosaurs to a dead end, he was frustrated. He felt responsible for all the dinosaurs. The dinosaurs felt defeated because they worked so hard, only to have to turn back.

This reminds me of the time that God led the Hebrews out of Egypt. God told Moses to have his people follow a special cloud. The cloud would lead them to safety. Moses trusted God and followed the cloud. But the cloud led them to a dead end, the Red Sea. The sea was too deep for the people to cross. The Egyptian armies were chasing them. The Hebrews were trapped.

Ask→
- How do you think the people felt?
- How do you think Moses felt?
- Can you think of a time when you tried to obey God but things just did not seem to work out?

Say→ Although it seemed that God had led Moses the wrong way, he did not. God split the Red Sea in two, and the Hebrews crossed safely to the other side. God knew what he was doing the whole time. God's ways are always right, even when they do not seem to make sense.

AWESOME DEEDS • Scripture: Exodus 13:17–14:31

Movie Title:
THE PRINCE OF EGYPT (G)

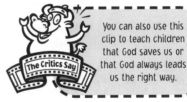

The Critics Say

You can also use this clip to teach children that God saves us or that God always leads us the right way.

Start Time: 1 hour, 26 minutes

Where to Begin: The man blows the trumpet.

Where to End: The silhouette of the great fish appears in the water.

Plot: Although Pharaoh released Moses and his people, he quickly changed his mind and mobilized an army to retake his slaves. Moses and the Hebrews are at the banks of the Red Sea. Their joy is interrupted when they see the Egyptian army bearing down on them. God instructs Moses to raise his staff. The sea splits and the people escape through a miraculous corridor.

Review: This clip dramatically captures the miraculous power of God. We can use this clip to help the children imagine what it must have been like to have lived through an amazing experience like crossing the Red Sea. We can teach them that God's power is completely amazing. Best yet, God is real and uses his power for the good of those who love him.

 Supplies: A large supply of old clothes, blankets, hats, and boots

NOW PLAYING

Have the children divide into groups of four.

Say→ **I want your groups to invent a new superhero. Make a costume for your hero with these clothes. Be sure to give your superhero a name as you dress him or her in the costume. You also need to give your superhero special powers so he or she can fight crime.**

Give the children five minutes to design their superheroes. Gather the children together, and let each group present its hero to the class.

Ask→ • **What would it be like to be friends with your superhero?**
• **If you were a superhero, how would you use your powers?**

Say→ **We like to imagine there are superheroes because of the special things they can do. In today's Bible story, we're going to see that God has amazing power—and that his power is real! Pharaoh has finally agreed to let the Israelites leave Egypt. They are no longer slaves. God led them to the edge of the Red Sea. But Pharaoh has changed his mind and wants to take the Israelites back. Let's see what happens.**

Show the *Prince of Egypt* movie clip.

Ask→ • **How did God show his power?**
• **How would you feel walking between two giant walls of water?**
• **What do you think the Egyptians thought about God's power after this day?**
• **How is God's power different from the power of a superhero?**
• **How do you feel knowing that God uses his power to help his people?**

Say→ **It's fun imagining superheroes. But God is better than superheroes because he is real!**

THE TEN COMMANDMENTS

A LITTLE SIN • *Scripture: Exodus 20:1-17*

 Movie Title:
VEGGIETALES: LARRY-BOY AND THE FIB FROM OUTER SPACE

You can also use this clip to teach children about sin or lying.

Start Time: 13 minutes, 23 seconds

Where to Begin: Laura and the others find Junior. Laura says, "There he is."

Where to End: Fib says, "A little fib couldn't hurt anybody."

Plot: When Junior breaks his father's collector's plate, a little blue fib from outer space ends up in Junior Asparagus' living room. The fib encourages Junior to tell a little lie. Junior agrees, and the fib grows out of control.

Review: Use this clip to help children see that God gives us rules for our good. Junior thought that a little lie wouldn't really matter, but eventually the lie grows out of control. Even "little" sins can grow into huge destructive forces that ruin our lives.

Supplies: Several wooden blocks, a small action figure, and a permanent marker

Preshow: Build a tower out of wooden blocks. Place the action figure at the top of the tower.

nOW PLAYING

Say→ We are going to watch a scene from *The Fib From Outer Space*. Junior accidentally broke his father's collectors plate. A little blue fib from outer space encouraged Junior to lie to his father about what happened. Junior decided to lie and the little fib grew a little bigger. Let's see what happens next with the fib.

Play the clip from *The Fib From Outer Space*.

Ask→ • Have you ever told a lie that caused problems for you later? What happened?
• Why do you think God wants us to always tell the truth?

Say→ One of the Ten Commandments found in the Bible tells us that "You shall not give false testimony against your neighbor." To give false testimony means to lie.

Sometimes we get tired of having rules that we have to obey. Let's play a game. First, I want you to name some rules that you have to live by. As the children name the rules, use the magic marker to write one rule on each block. Have the children make a tower out of the blocks. Set the action figure on top of the tower. Say: **This man is like you and me. When we obey the rules God gave us, we stand tall. Let's see what happens if we try to live without rules.**

Let the children take turns trying to remove a block, one by one, without knocking down the tower. When the tower collapses, have the children discuss the following questions.

Ask→ • How is this game like what life would be like without rules?
• Why do you think our parents give us rules?
• Why do you think God gives us rules?

Say→ God gave us these rules so we don't hurt each other or ourselves.

Movie Clip:
THE LION, THE WITCH, AND THE WARDROBE (NOT RATED)

Start Time: 37 minutes, 10 seconds

Where to Begin: Lucy says, "Tell us about Aslan."

Where to End: The He-Beaver says, "Safe? Of course it isn't safe. But he's good."

You can also use this clip to teach children about sharing their faith.

Plot: The children have entered the world of Narnia and are eating a meal with the Beaver family. The Beavers are trying to explain who the great and wonderful Aslan is to the children.

Review: The Narnia Series was written by theologian C.S. Lewis. Lewis' *Chronicles of Narnia* is crammed with allegories designed to help children (and their adults) grasp Christian truth. Aslan is the series' Christ-character. You can use this clip to help children understand the awe and reverence that should accompany any talk of God. Just as the Beavers spoke with respect and honor, our children can learn to treat God's name with respect and honor. The essence of this commandment is that we use God's name with reverence.

Supplies: A Bible, a chalkboard and chalk or newsprint and a marker

NOW PLAYING

Play a guessing game with the children. Whisper the name of a celebrity or well-known TV character to a child. Have that children draw pictures to try to get the others to guess the mystery celebrity. The child may not use words. Play several rounds, giving a number of children a chance to draw clues to the mystery celebrity.

Ask➜ • Was it easy or hard to get people to guess whom your mystery person was?
• What was your strategy?

Say➜ Let's watch a movie clip from *The Lion, the Witch, and the Wardrobe*. In the movie, four children have entered a marvelous land called Narnia. The children are having dinner with talking Beavers. The Beavers are trying to explain whom a person named Aslan was and what he was like. The children have never met Aslan. Watch what happens.

Play the *Lion, the Witch, and the Wardrobe* clip.

Ask➜ • How do the Beavers feel about Aslan?
• What about their words helps you make that conclusion?
• If the Beavers had said mean things about Aslan, what kind of impression would the children have of Aslan?

Read Exodus 20:7.

Say→ One of the Ten Commandments tells us to talk about God's name respectfully.

Ask→
- Why do you think God made this rule?
- Pretend you had a friend who did not know God, and you used God's name badly. Maybe you used God's name as part of a swear word. How special do you think your friends would think God is?
- How can we talk about God to let people know we think he is special?

THE FALL OF JERICHO

GOD'S WAYS ARE BEST • Scripture: Joshua 5:13–6:27

 Movie Title:
VEGGIETALES: JOSH AND THE BIG WALL

You can also use this clip to teach children about peer pressure or good choices.

Start Time: 19 minutes, 48 seconds

Where to Begin: The narrator says, "Those are very interesting instructions."

Where to End: The narrator says, "Oh no, it looks like they are going to disobey God again."

Plot: The children of Israel have been following God's seemingly odd instructions for the siege of Jericho. God has told them to simply march around the wall for days. The army comes back to the camp. Dissension breaks out and several alternate plans are discussed.

Review: We can use this clip to teach children that we should obey God, even when his will doesn't seem to make sense. Children constantly have to choose between God's way and the wrong way. We can show the children that God's ways are always right.

 Supplies: Blindfolds and a plate of treats

NOW PLAYING

Have the class form groups of three. Have one person in each group wear the blindfold over his or her eyes. Assign one member to be the "Guide." Have the final member be the "Deceiver." Set the plate of treats on the opposite side of the room. Instruct the Guide to lead the blindfolded partner to the treats by using words. The Deceiver's job is to steer the blindfolded person away from the snacks. Neither the Guide nor the Deceiver may touch the blindfolded person. This way the blindfolded child must rely on his or her ability to pick out the right voice. Let the children play until most of the blindfolded children make it to the treats. Instruct children to take off their blindfolds. Hand everyone a treat for playing a great game.

Ask→ • If you were blindfolded, how did you know who to listen to?

• How did it feel to have two different directions being given to you at the same time?

Say→ This reminds me of a Bible story. God had given the children of Israel some interesting instructions to conquer the city of Jericho. Jericho had big walls around it. Normally, you would have to fight your way into the city. But God had a different plan. God told the people to march around the city once a day for six days. On the seventh day, they were supposed to march around the city seven times. Let's watch this scene from *Josh and the Big Wall* to see what a conversation back at the Israelite camp might have been like between days of marching.

Show the *Josh and the Big Wall* clip.

Ask→ • Why do you think people were coming up with plans that were different from God's plan?

• Have you ever been tempted to do something that God did not want you to do because God's ways did not seem to make sense?

• Can you think of some of God's rules that are hard to understand?

Say→ Joshua and his people did choose to follow God's plan. They listened to God's plan instead of their own plans—just as the blindfolded players listened to the Guide's voice instead of the Deceiver's voice. On the seventh day, they marched around the walls seven times. They blew their trumpets, and the walls of the city came falling down! God's ways are best.

CHOOSING SIDES • *Scripture: Joshua 5:13–6:27*

Movie Title:
SPACE JAM (PG)

Start Time: 55 minutes, 11 seconds

Where to Begin: The mouse announces the starting line up.

You can also use this clip to teach children about the importance of teamwork or about courage in the face of impossible odds.

The Critics Say

Where to End: The Tasmanian Devil passes out.

Plot: A cast of cartoon characters has enlisted Michael Jordan to help them beat a team of formidable aliens who have stolen the basketball talent from the NBA's finest. This clip illustrates what an obvious mismatch the game would be if Michael Jordan were not on their side.

Review: You can use this clip to help children understand the importance of being on God's side. Joshua was about to lead his army to lay siege to a walled city in a land populated with giants. Joshua had every reason to be intimidated. The people of Jericho had every tactical advantage—a walled city, knowledge of the terrain, and giants. However, Joshua knew the Israelites were on God's team. With God on their team, no one could stand against them.

Supplies: Several packs of basketball cards, a white T-shirt, and a fabric marker

now PLAYING

Say→ **Here are some basketball cards. Pretend you are building a "dream team." Pick the players you would want to have on your team.** Pass out the packs of cards. Let the children sort through the cards and select who they think are the best players.

Ask→ • **How did you decide who you wanted on your team?**
• **How would it feel to play ball with these players?**

Say→ **We're going to watch a scene where The Looney Tunes have to play a team of space aliens that stole their basketball talent from the best of the professional basketball players. Tell me if you think the teams are fair.**

Play the *Space Jam* movie clip.

> **The Critics Say**
> Be sure to include packs of WNBA cards to help the girls in the class relate to the activity. These cards are a little harder to get but they should be available at most sports card stores.

Ask→ • **Do you think the teams are fair? Why or why not?**

Say→ **In the Bible, there is a story about a general named Joshua. Joshua had to lead his people to fight a mighty people. They had a big city named Jericho that had big walls surrounding it. One night, Joshua was taking a walk. The commander of the Lord appeared to him. Joshua asked if the commander was on his side. The commander said that he was on God's side. Joshua humbled himself and listened to what the commander had to say.**

Ask→ • **Why did Joshua decide to listen to the commander?**
• **What does it mean to be on the Lord's side?**

Hold up the T-shirt.

Say→ **In basketball, players wear uniforms to help people know what team they are on. Let's make a uniform for someone who is on God's side. What does someone who is on God's side look like? For example, you might say that he or she prays.**

Write down the children's suggestions on the jersey with the fabric marker. When the children are finished, lead the children in praying that they would live lives that would let everyone know they are on God's side.

SAMSON AND DELILAH

DISAPPEARING POWERS • Scripture: Judges 16:1-31

The Critics Say: You can use this clip to teach children about self-esteem, persistence, and the need to trust in God.

Movie Title:
ROOKIE OF THE YEAR (PG)

Start Time: 1 hour, 25 minutes, 30 seconds

Where to Begin: Henry is throwing very fast pitches.

Where to End: Henry tries to throw after falling on his arm, and says, "Oh no, it's all over."

Plot: A young boy named Henry has incredible strength throwing a baseball after his broken arm heals. In one quick accident on the field, all his power is taken away from him, and he must find the strength to go on.

Review: You can use this scene to help children see that things may happen to us to change us, but we can always have faith in ourselves and in God. In the Bible, Samson lost his strength when his hair was cut. In the movie clip, Henry loses his strength after falling on his arm. One small action made a big difference in each person's life, but they each kept their faith.

Supplies: Bowls of water, bowls of flour, small marbles, and paper towels

Preshow: Set out bowls of water and flour so that each pair in your class can reach them.

NOW PLAYING

Say→ I want you to find a partner and sit across from him or her on the floor. The partner who has the longest hair can come up and get a marble from me. I want you to dip your marble in a bowl of water and then gently roll it to your partner. Let children roll the marbles back and forth for a couple of minutes.

Ask→ • Was it easy to roll and catch the wet marble?
• What is one thing you could change about the marble that would make it harder to roll?

Say→ I have an idea of how we could take some of the power away from the marble, but first I want to show you a video clip. This clip is from the movie *Rookie of the Year*. It shows a young boy losing all of his pitching strength when he falls. Let's watch and see if we can think of a Bible story in which someone loses all of his strength from one event.

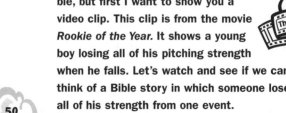

The Critics Say: If you have children under five, use balls instead of marbles (marbles are a choking risk). If you have carpeting, lay some paper down for rolling so the flour is easier to clean up.

Show the *Rookie of the Year* clip.

Ask➜ • **How do you think Henry felt when he found out he had lost most of his pitching strength?**

Say➜ **In the Bible, Samson lost most of his strength when he disobeyed God and his hair was cut. With your partner across from you, get your marble wet and roll it in the bowl of flour. Try and roll the marble to your partner. Let's see how changing one thing can make a difference to the power of our marble rolling.** Let children try rolling the marbles back and forth a few times. Make sure they keep enough flour on the marbles to cause resistance.

Ask➜ • **What happened when you changed one thing with your rolling marble?**
• **How is this like what happened to Henry or Samson?**

Say➜ **I want you to roll your marble one more time in the water to wash off the flour. As you roll it to your partner, tell him or her about how God has helped you do something you couldn't do on your own.** Let children roll the marbles one last time. **No matter how strong or good we are at something, we always need God's help. God is always happy to help us when we put our faith and trust in him.**

HIDDEN STRENGTH • Scripture: Judges 16:1-31

Movie Title:
THE PRINCESS BRIDE (PG)

Start Time: 21 minutes, 33 seconds

Where to Begin: Westley prepares for the sword duel with Inigo saying, "You've been more than fair."

You can use this clip to teach children about hard work, sportsmanship, spiritual gifts, and doing their best.

The Critics Say

Where to End: Westley wins the duel.

Plot: Buttercup has been kidnapped by a group of talented but unbalanced criminals. Her masked love, Westley comes to her rescue and must face each of the criminals along the way. Westley's first challenge is a duel with the misguided but kindhearted master swordsman, Inigo Montoya. Both men start the duel using their weaker left hands, and Westley wins the fight.

Review: Both Inigo and Westley are master sword fighters. Inigo begins the duel using his left hand to make the fight interesting. During the fight, he is amazed to learn that Westley was using his weaker left hand also. Like Samson, Westley had amazing hidden power. While the children in your class may not be able to sword fight or catch foxes by the tail, they have amazing power because the Holy Spirit is with them.

NOW PLAYING

Demonstrate a special hidden talent you have. For example, you might be able to blow a big bubble or cross your eyes. Give each child an opportunity to demonstrate his or her special hidden talent for the class.

Say→ We're going to watch a short movie clip about two men who have a special talent. As you watch, try to see how the men hide their talent. Let's watch.

Show the movie clip from *The Princess Bride*.

Ask→ • What special talent did the two men have?
  • How did they try to hide their talents?

Say→ There was a man in the Bible named Samson who had a special talent.

Ask→ • Does anyone know what his special talent was?
  • What was the secret of Samson's strength?

Briefly summarize the story of Samson.

Say→ We all have special gifts and abilities. Our talents come from God, just as Samson's strength came from God. Let's use our talents to glorify God!

THE LORD CALLS SAMUEL

WHAT'S THAT? • *Scripture: 1 Samuel 3:1-21*

 Movie Title:
THE LION KING (G)

Start Time: 1 hour, 4 minutes, 44 seconds

Where to Begin: Simba is asking Raffiki if he knew his father.

You can use this clip to teach children about honoring our parents and listening to and following God's Word.

Where to End: Simba is chasing Raffiki away with a stick after seeing his vision in the sky.

Plot: Simba is alone and not sure what to do. His dead father, Mufasa, forms a shape in the sky, and tells him that he needs to follow his destiny to be the real king. He needs to remember who he is. He is his father's son. This encounter gives Simba strength to go on and defeat Scar.

Review: We are God's children, and God communicates with and leads his children. Simba found direction as his father spoke to him in the sky. Children may be expecting a similar

Some Christians see Raffiki as a shaman. If you don't have time to help children understand a biblical perspective on this issue, you may not want to show this clip to your kids. It's also best to use this clip with older children, who are able to understand that God (or our friends and family) doesn't talk to us through the stars.

experience when they hear the story of Samuel. While God can use whatever methods he chooses, help your children see that God does in fact clearly communicate with them now through the Bible.

NOW PLAYING

Say→ We're going to watch a scene from *The Lion King*. Simba is alone and not sure what to do. Raffiki the baboon helps him find his father. Let's see what Simba's father tells him.

Show the *Lion King* clip.

Ask→ • How do you think Simba felt when he heard his father giving him advice?
• Do you think it was easy for Simba to follow his father's words? Why or why not?
• Can you tell us about a time when it was hard to follow someone's advice?

Say→ Simba really needed some direction in his life. In this pretend story, his dad told him what to do. Let me tell you a true story about someone who needed direction.

In the Bible, there was a boy named Samuel who thought that he heard the priest Eli speaking to him. It was God telling him things he needed to know.

I want you to find a partner. Now "draw" a letter from your name on your partner's back. See if your partner can tell what letter you are drawing. Try another letter. If you want, you can also try spelling a short word on your partner's back. When you're done, switch places, and let your partner try sending you a message.

Ask→ • How did it feel when you understood your partner's message?
• How did it feel when you got the message wrong?

Say→ Samuel did not understand at first that it was God speaking to him. It took Samuel three times before he realized that God was actually trying to communicate to him.

We don't need to look to the stars to get direction—we won't find any direction there anyway. God may or may not call us like he called Samuel. But we know we can find God's direction anytime we need it. God's words to us are found in the Bible. We can always go to the Bible when we need God's direction and we can always pray asking God to show us the way to go—and God will answer our prayer!

FOLLOW GOD'S DIRECTION • Scripture: 1 Samuel 3:1-21

Movie Title:
LEAVE IT TO BEAVER (PG)

Start Time: 19 minutes, 30 seconds

Where to Begin: Beaver is showing a stranger his new bike.

The Critics Say

You can use this clip to teach children about following God's Word or the difference between good directions and bad directions.

Where to End: Beaver is running after his stolen bike and pauses as it disappears.

Plot: Beaver was given bad directions from a boy wanting to take his bike. By listening to the boy, Beaver got his bike stolen.

Review: Sometimes people can give us bad directions or lead us into trouble. Beaver accepted bad directions from a boy who wanted to steal his bike. Samuel also accepted directions, but they were directions from God. When God tells us to do things, it may not always be easy, but it is always for our good.

 Supplies: Dimes and drinking straws

NOW PLAYING

Give each child a dime.

Say➜ **I want you to try and pick up the dime without touching it with any part of your body and without using any metal, wood, or cardboard instrument.** Let children try for a few minutes.

Ask➜ • **Have you ever been given bad or wrong directions?**
• **What happened?**

Say➜ **I have a movie clip from** *Leave It to Beaver.* **Beaver gets some bad directions. Let's see what happens.**

Show the *Leave It to Beaver* movie clip.

Ask➜ • **Why did that boy give Beaver bad directions?**

Make straws available to your students.

Say➜ **God always gives only good directions. In the Bible, a boy named Samuel also got some directions. His directions were from God. I think I could be more helpful to you now and give you some better directions with your dime. Place a straw against your dime and suck up the air from the other end. Now you should be able to pick up your dime.** Let children try using the straw and the new directions you provided.

Ask➜ • **Where can we find directions from God?**

DAVID AND GOLIATH

WE CAN DO IT • *Scripture: 1 Samuel 17:1-50*

Movie Title:
THE BIG GREEN (PG)

Start Time: 1 hour, 30 minutes, 45 seconds

You can use this clip to teach children to overcome obstacles or to trust in God.

The Critics Say

Where to Begin: The coach is announcing with a megaphone that his son will play the final part of the soccer game.

Where to End: The Big Green team wins the final championship, and the crowd erupts.

Plot: A team of soccer misfits become local heroes when the goalie gathers his strength and blocks the goal, and the smallest boy on the Big Green team scores a goal to win the game.

Review: You can use this scene to show two examples of how children can be afraid to face their opponents in situations that may seem too hard for them. The crowd didn't think the two boys could defeat their formidable opponent, but the small boys found the strength to defeat their opponents and win the game. In 1 Samuel 17, David faced a similar problem when he fought Goliath. Despite his size and age, David trusted in God and was victorious.

Supplies: Cups of water and paper towels

Preshow: For each child, fill one cup of water halfway.

now PLAYING

Say→ Tell me about a time when you had to do something that seemed impossible. How did you feel when you did it?

I have something for you to try that may seem hard to do. I want you to get a few drops of water out of your cup without touching or blowing on the cup. Give each child a cup of water and a paper towel. Let the children try for a couple of minutes. Now I want you to put a rolled up piece of paper towel in the water so it hangs out over the edge of the cup. I have a fun movie clip that we can watch, while we wait to get back to our cups.

In this movie, called *The Big Green,* two boys have to do something that seems impossible, and the crowd doesn't think they can do it. Let's see if they can do something that seems hard to do.

Show the *Big Green* clip.

Say→ Now squeeze the paper towel that is hanging out from the cup. In the Bible, David also had to do what seemed impossible. He fought a giant named Goliath that many people were afraid of. He knew that God would be with him while he tried to do something hard. When God is with us, we can do things that seem very hard for us to do.

Some of you may have found ways to get water out of the cup. Some of you may have found it impossible. We came up with a really easy solution by using the paper towel. Our impossible situations are easy for God to solve. So next time you have to face something that's impossible, ask for God to help you!

Movie Title:

THE JUNGLE BOOK (ANIMATED, 1967) (NOT RATED)

The Critics Say

Use this clip to teach children about courage, bullies, or conflict.

Start Time: 1 hour, 5 minutes, 58 seconds

Where to Begin: Sher Kan says, "That's what friends are for."

Where to End: Sher Kan says, "Ten."

Plot: Sher Kan, the tiger, has been trying to find the Man Cub, Mowgli. Mowgli's friends have been trying to take him to the man village to keep him safe from Sher Kan, but Mowgli has been protesting. He informs his friends that he is in no way, shape, or form afraid of Sher Kan. When Mowgli and Sher Kan finally come face to face, Mowgli stands up to Sher Kan.

Review: You can use this scene to help the children understand how we can all face giants when we have God on our side. David was facing a giant, but he was not afraid because he knew he had God on his side. Likewise, Mowgli was facing a giant and should have been afraid of Sher Kan. Everyone else in the movie was intimidated by him and avoided him at all costs. Mowgli, on the other hand, was almost eager to meet Sher Kan and fight him. Similarly, David was undaunted by Goliath's size and strength.

Supplies: Overhead projector, overhead transparency, overhead markers, newspaper, and tape measure

Preshow: Before class, photocopy the sample Goliath (p. 57) onto one of the transparencies. Place the projector in an area of the room that will allow you to project the Goliath transparency onto the wall and make him over nine feet tall. Use the tape measure to get an accurate measurement.

NOW PLAYING

Say→ We're going to watch a scene from *The Jungle Book.* Mowgli and Sher Kan have finally come face to face, and Sher Kan is expecting Mowgli to run away in fear. Let's watch.

The Critics Say

If you don't have a transparency that can be used in a photocopier, you can just draw a stick-figure Goliath on a transparency to be used during the activity.

Show the *Jungle Book* clip.

Ask→ • How do you think Sher Kan felt when Mowgli stood up to him and didn't run away?

• What do you think made Mowgli so brave?

Use this picture of Goliath for the "Giant Fighting" activity.

Say→ Have you ever heard the story of the young boy David and the giant Goliath? I have a picture of Goliath I'd like to show you.

Shine the picture of Goliath up on the wall.

Say→ The Bible tells us that Goliath was over nine feet tall. This is about how tall Goliath would have been. I want you all to come and take a turn measuring yourself against Goliath.

Give each child a chance to stand next to Goliath.

Say→ Goliath was a part of the Philistine army that was fighting against the Israelites. David was a part of the Israelite army. Everyone in the Israelite army was afraid to fight Goliath, but not David. David volunteered to fight Goliath, and David won! He used a stone, a slingshot, and his faith in God to beat the mighty giant. I'm going to give you each a piece of newspaper, and I want you to wad it up. Now on the count of three, I want you to throw your newspaper stone at Goliath's forehead.

Count to three, and let the children try to hit Goliath in the forehead with their paper stones.

Ask→ • How were Mowgli and David alike?
• How were they different?

Say→ David fought Goliath with stones and God's help. We sometimes feel as we have giants we need to fight.

Isn't it great to know that God will help us face all the giants in our lives, and he will help us defeat them, just as God helped David defeat Goliath.

DAVID AND JONATHAN

PROTECTION • *Scripture: 1 Samuel 20:1-42*

 Movie Title:
SLEEPING BEAUTY (NOT RATED)

You can use this clip to teach children about protection or friendship.

The Critics Say

Start Time: 12 minutes

Where to Begin: Flora says, "I'll turn her into a flower."

Where to End: The three fairies run down the hill.

Plot: A princess named Aurora has been born and everyone in the kingdom has gathered to welcome her. The three good fairies have all prepared a special gift for the princess, but before the third fairy can give her gift to Aurora, Maleficent the evil empress, curses Aurora. Everyone in the kingdom is distraught over the curse and plans are taken to protect the princess and keep the curse from being carried out.

Review: You can use this scene to help children understand that God can use others to protect us from people or things that may harm us.

In the movie, the three fairies are trying everything they can think of to keep Princess Aurora from the evil Maleficent. Likewise, Jonathan came up with a plan to protect David from Jonathan's father, King Saul.

Preshow: Prepare a descriptive list of people who try to protect and keep us from harm. The list could include parents, pastors, teachers, doctors, police officers, and firefighters. Also include five to ten descriptive words or phrases about each person. For example, descriptive words for a doctor might be "white coat, office or hospital, when you're sick, shots, and medicine."

> The Critics Say
>
> If you feel parents of children in your class may object to movies that have fairies or magic, you may not want to show this clip to your class.

Now PLAYING

Say→ We're going to play a guessing game. I'm going to give you clues about different people who protect you and keep you from harm. When you think you know whom I'm describing, stand up, but don't say the answer.

Choose one of the people on your list, and begin giving the clues one at a time. Then have children shout out whom you are describing. Continue to play until you have described everyone on your list.

Say→ In our game, we were trying to figure out different people who try to protect us from harm. We're going to watch a scene from *Sleeping Beauty*. The three good fairies are trying to come up with a way to protect Aurora from the evil Maleficent. Let's watch.

Show the *Sleeping Beauty* clip.

Ask→ • How did the three fairies try to protect Princess Aurora?
• Why do you think the fairies were willing to sacrifice so much to save the princess?

Say→ The Bible tells us about two friends named Jonathan and David. Jonathan's father, King Saul, loved David, but then he became jealous of David and wanted to harm him. Jonathan promised David that he would help him escape. Jonathan devised a plan that would allow David to know if the rumors were true and King Saul was trying to harm him. When the truth was found out, Jonathan was sad to have to send his friend away. David was brokenhearted that he had to leave his friend, but was thankful that God had provided someone he could trust to help him escape.

Ask→ • How is what the fairies did for Princess Aurora like what Jonathan did for David?
• How is it different?
• Who is someone in your life that tries to protect you from things that may harm you?

Movie Title:

POOH'S GRAND ADVENTURE: THE SEARCH FOR CHRISTOPHER ROBIN (NOT RATED)

Start Time: 5 minutes, 21 seconds

Where to Begin: Christopher Robin says, "Pooh Bear, what if some day there came a tomorrow when we were apart?"

> **The Critics Say**
>
> You can use this clip to teach children about friendship, loyalty, or change.

Where to End: Christopher Robin says, "I'll always be with you, I'll always be with you, always be with you."

Plot: Winnie the Pooh and Christopher Robin are doing what best friends do best, spending time together. They are enjoying one another's company, but Christopher Robin poses a serious question when he asks what would happen if there ever came a day when they were no longer together. Winnie the Pooh explains that that day will never come.

Review: You can use this scene to help the children understand the special bond between David and Jonathan. Just like Winnie the Pooh and Christopher Robin are best friends in the movie, David and Jonathan were best friends. They loved one another as brothers. When the day came for David to leave, Jonathan and David vowed that they would be friends forever, even if they were apart.

Supplies: Newsprint, markers, and tape

Preshow: Cut one six-foot piece of newsprint for every four students in your class.

NOW PLAYING

Have children form groups of four. Have one child lay down on a large sheet of newsprint, and another child trace around him or her. Encourage the children to draw facial features and clothing on the body outlines. Tell the children that the people they've drawn are ideal friends. Have them write characteristics or qualities they want in a friend all around the body outlines.

> **The Critics Say**
>
> If you have a small class, you could allow each student to make his or her own ideal friend. If you have a class of younger students who don't read or write well, you can write the characteristics for them when they are finished coloring their ideal friends.

Say→ **We're going to watch a scene from *Pooh's Grand Adventure: The Search for Christopher Robin*. Winnie the Pooh and Christopher Robin are enjoying the day together when Christopher**

Robin asks Pooh a rather serious question. Let's watch and see what happens.

Show the *Pooh's Grand Adventure* clip.

Ask→
- **What did Christopher Robin ask Winnie the Pooh?**
- **What was Winnie the Pooh's response?**
- **How did Christopher Robin respond to Pooh?**

Say→ In 1 Samuel there's a story about a man named Jonathan and his best friend, David. Jonathan and David had promised to be friends forever. They enjoyed spending time with one another, they trusted one another, and they counted on one another in times of need. Jonathan's father, King Saul, became jealous and wanted to hurt David.

Jonathan wanted to help David, so he came up with a plan to save David from King Saul's anger and jealousy. Jonathan was a true friend to David. He was willing to go against his father and even risk his own life to spare David's. In the end, when David had to leave for his own safety, Jonathan and David renewed the promise to be friends forever, even if they were apart.

Ask→
- **How is Jonathan and David's friendship like Winnie the Pooh and Christopher Robin's?**
- **Can you name someone in your life that is a good friend as Jonathan was to David?**
- **What makes a good friend?**

Allow the children a couple of more minutes to add more characteristics of a good friend, then hang the ideal friend outlines around the room.

ELIJAH AND THE PROPHETS OF BAAL

THE CONTEST • *Scripture: 1 Kings 18:16–39*

Movie Title:
ROBIN HOOD (ANIMATED, 1973) (G)

You can use this clip to teach children about cheating and competition.

The Critics Say

Start Time: 40 minutes

Where to Begin: The Alligator says, "For the final shoot out..."

Where to End: Maid Marion hugs her handmaiden.

Plot: Robin Hood has come in disguise to compete in the archery contest. The contest is a trap set up by Prince John to capture Robin Hood. In the final round, Robin Hood competes against the Sheriff of Nottingham.

Review: You can use this scene to help children understand that when you have God on your side you don't have to cheat or go to extremes to win. Elijah was faced with the task of bringing the people back to God after they had turned to false gods. Elijah set up a contest to prove that God is the only true God.

In the Robin Hood clip, the Sheriff of Nottingham is willing to do anything he has to in order to win the competition, even cheat if necessary. The prophets of Baal go to extremes also, cutting themselves in hope of their gods answering. With God's help, Elijah prevails, and the people realize the true God is greater than all others.

Supplies: Edible "building supplies" such as marshmallows, pretzel sticks, gumdrops, and jelly beans

Preshow: Divide the building supplies into equal amounts for groups of four.

now PLAYING

Say→ We're going to watch a scene from *Robin Hood*. Robin Hood is competing against the Sheriff of Nottingham in an archery contest. Let's watch.

Show the *Robin Hood* clip.

Ask→ • Why do you think the Sheriff of Nottingham was willing to cheat to win?
• Did his cheating help him win?

Say→ There is a story in the Bible about a man named Elijah. Elijah was the only prophet of God left and almost all the people had forgotten about God. The people were following the false gods of the prophets of Baal. Elijah thought of a way to show the people who the true God was. He set up a contest with the prophets of Baal. Before I tell you the rest of the story, I'm going to divide you into teams, and you're going to make "altars."

Have children wash their hands and then form groups of four. Give each group the edible building supplies. Tell them not to eat the supplies as they work. Give groups several minutes to work to build an altar. Give a definition of an altar if needed.

Say→ Elijah told the prophets of Baal to set up an altar and pray to their gods to send down a fire to burn the offering that was on the altar. The prophets cried out to their gods with no luck. They yelled and screamed and even scraped themselves trying to get their gods to listen.

When Elijah took his turn, he poured water on the altar first. Then he prayed to God, and God sent down a fire that burnt up the offering, the altar, and all the water that had been poured over it. Elijah knew that his God was the one and only true God. After seeing this competition, the people turned back to God.

Ask→ • How were the prophets of Baal and the Sheriff of Nottingham alike?
• How were Robin Hood and Elijah alike?
• What were the differences between these two people?

Say→ Elijah knew that he would win the contest because he had God on his side. God won't necessarily help you win games or make your team win. But God will help you when you are trying to do what is right and are trying to do God's will.

Let the children "consume" their altars by eating them.

Movie Title:
MULAN (G)

Start Time: 54 minutes

Where to Begin: The Captain says, "Hold the last cannon."

The Critics Say

> You can use this clip to teach children about courage, God's help, or facing challenges.

Where to End: The three soldiers run and hide behind the rock, and the snow goes over them.

Plot: Ping (Mulan) and the other soldiers have been fighting against the Huns. They think they have defeated them, only to find out they haven't! Ping makes the choice to continue to fight the Huns, even when the other soldiers run and the odds seem too great.

Review: You can use this scene to help children understand that even when they feel they are outnumbered, if God is on their side, they have all the help they'll ever need. Elijah was the only prophet of God left. There were 450 prophets of Baal and 400 prophets of Asherah. Only a remnant of the people believed in God, and most were following the false prophets. Elijah knew this was wrong and knew that he had to bring the people back to a relationship with God. Elijah knew that even though he was outnumbered, he had God on his side and he would win.

Supplies: Ten balloons, masking tape, and a blindfold for each child

Preshow: Inflate the balloons, and use the masking tape to create a volley-ball court on the floor in your room.

NOW PLAYING

To begin, have the chosen child go to one side of the court and all the other children to the other side.

The Critics Say

> For this game, choose a confident child to be the lone player.

Say→ **We will be playing balloon volleyball. If the balloon touches the ground on your team's side, the other team gets a point. We will play to five points.**

Give the team with the majority of the students all the balloons and allow them to serve them all at the same time. Obviously, the odds will be too great for the solo child, and the five points will be scored quickly.

Say→ **Now let's change the game. Each of you on the big team will put on a blind-fold and sit down to play. We will play to five points again.**

Blindfold each member of the big team, tell them they must keep their arms at their sides, and give the balloons to the solo child. Allow him to serve as many balloons at a time as he chooses.

Say→ **We're going to watch a scene from *Mulan*. Ping and the other soldiers**

have been fighting against the Huns, and they think they have defeated them. When they find out they haven't, Ping does something amazing. Let's watch.

> Show the *Mulan* clip.

Ask→ • How do you think the soldiers felt when they realized the Huns were coming after them?

• Why do you think Ping decided to fight the Huns alone?

Say→ In 1 Kings there's a story about a man named Elijah. Elijah was one of the only prophets of God left. Most of the people had stopped following God, and Elijah knew that this was not what God wanted. Elijah decided that even though there was only one of him and 450 prophets of Baal and 400 prophets of Asherah, he would challenge them to prove their gods were fake. The odds against Elijah were great, 850 to 1! Elijah knew that he had the true God on his side, and he would be the winner.

Ask→ • How were Ping and Elijah's situations alike?

• How were the situations different?

• Have you ever been in a situation where you felt outnumbered?

Say→ Maybe you've felt as if you're the only one who wants to do what is right. Or maybe you are the only one in your class who goes to church. It is easy to feel outnumbered in those situations. The next time you get in a situation where you feel as if you're the only one, remember Elijah. Put your trust in God, and the two of you will outnumber them all!

ESTHER'S REQUEST

RELUCTANT HERO • Scripture: Esther 5:1-7; 7:1-7

Movie Title:
🎥 THE RESCUERS (G)

Start Time: 26 minutes, 55 seconds

Where to Begin: Miss Bianca enters the meeting of the Rescue Aid Society to discuss Penny's rescue.

The Critics Say

You can use this clip to teach children about teamwork and courage.

Where to End: The other delegates cheer Miss Bianca's selection of Bernard to accompany her on the rescue mission.

Plot: The Rescue Aid Society, an organization made up of mice from all over the world, gets an urgent message to rescue an orphan named Penny from Madame Medusa. The confident Miss Bianca volunteers immediately for the

The Critics Say

Kids often feel like they're inadequate artists. Assure children that they simply need to do their best.

rescue operation. She then volunteers Bernard, a janitor mouse who (like Esther) is reluctant and skeptical of the role he can play in helping anyone.

Review: You can use this scene from *The Rescuers* to help children understand how Esther was faithful to do what God called her to do, even though she, like Bernard, was afraid.

Supplies: Paper and markers

now playing

Divide the class into two groups. Assign Esther 5:1-7 to group 1 and Esther 7:1-7 to group 2. In each group have an older elementary student or a helper read the passage. Give children paper and markers. Have each child in group 1 illustrate something he or she would like to ask the U.S. president to help them do to help others. It may be distributing food to poor people, providing jobs to those who need them, or helping people learn to read. Encourage kids to think big.

Have children in group 2 each illustrate something that they would like to ask their school principals to help them do to help others at school. Their illustrations may show tutors helping children who struggle with learning, school lunches being served to those who can't afford them, or an after-school program for those who go home to an empty house. Again encourage kids to think big. After allowing time for kids to create, have them share their illustrations with the whole group.

Say→ We're going to watch a scene from *The Rescuers.* The Rescue Aid Society has found an urgent message from an orphan named Penny. The Rescue Aid Society is looking for volunteers to rescue Penny. Let's watch.

Show *The Rescuers* clip.

Ask→ • Why do you think that Bernard was nervous about going on the mission to rescue Penny?

• What do you think Miss Bianca saw in Bernard that made her want Bernard as her partner?

Say→ Sometimes we don't feel capable of doing anything for God. Esther needed to ask the king to stop Haman from killing the Jewish people. Esther was afraid to face the king. In that day, people who came to the king without being asked were often killed or punished. Even though she was afraid, Esther asked the king for help.

Ask→ • How are Miss Bianca and Bernard's mission to rescue Penny like Esther's mission to rescue her people?

• Have any of you had the experience of having to do something difficult for God?

• What can you do to serve God?

Have children look at the illustrations they have made and consider selecting one act of service that they can do together.

Movie Title:

MCGEE & ME! THE BIG LIE (PUBLISHED BY FOCUS ON THE FAMILY AND DISTRIBUTED BY TYNDALE CHRISTIAN VIDEO)

Start Time: 5 minutes, 45 seconds

Where to Begin: Nick is walking home from school and is confronted by bullies.

Where to End: Nick begins to take a short cut home after Louis rescues him.

> **The Critics Say**
>
> You can use this clip to teach children about respecting others, God's care, and helping others.

Plot: The main character, Nick, has moved to a new home and has started at a new school. While walking home from school, he is confronted by bullies but saved by his new friend Louis.

Review: You can use this scene to help children understand that sometimes we have to take a stand for God. Louis had to help Nick stand against some bullies, just as Esther had to stand up against Haman to save God's people.

Supplies: A Bible and masking tape

Preshow: Use the masking tape to make a starting line.

NOW PLAYING

Have children play this game similar to Mother May I. Stand at the front of the room. Have kids line up at the starting line at the other end of the room. Each child must request to take three steps and begin the request with the words "May I." For example, a child might say, "May I take a skip, a giant step, and a baby step?" Grant the request by saying, "Yes, you may." If the child fails to start the request with "May I," send him or her back to the starting line. You also have the power to change a request. For example, if a child correctly requests three giant steps you may say, "No, you may not, but you may take a jump and two giant steps." Play the game until each child has had three or four opportunities to make a request.

> **The Critics Say**
>
> Have fun with this game, and don't worry about declaring a winner. Play your role in true "royal" fashion. For example, if kids forget to say "May I," "demand" that they return to the starting line. You might also act very put out when you deny correctly spoken requests and "grant" new sets of steps for them to take.

Ask→
- **In our game did I treat you all fairly?**
- **How did you feel while waiting for my decision to your requests?**
- **What do you think it would be like to make a request to a real king?**

Say→ In the book of Esther, we find a decree had been signed which would result in the death of many Jews. Though Esther was the queen, she could not approach the king unless he raised his royal scepter. Read Esther 7:1-7.

We're going to watch a scene from *The Big Lie* where someone sticks up for another person in trouble. Nick is new to the area and walks down an alley where some bullies hang out. Let's watch.

Show the *McGee and Me!* clip.

Say→ Like Louis who had to stand up to the bullies to protect Nick, Queen Esther had to stand up to the king for her people. The King found favor with Queen Esther and allowed the queen to host a banquet for him. At that banquet, Esther requested that her people be spared.

Ask→ • How difficult do you think it was for Esther to go before the king?
• Why do you think Louis in *The Big Lie* was so brave?

Say→ If you ask God for help, he will always give you the courage to do the right thing.

THE LORD IS MY SHEPHERD (PSALM 23)

RESCUE SHEPHERD • *Scripture: Psalm 23*

Movie Title:
FAR FROM HOME: THE ADVENTURES OF YELLOW DOG (PG)

Start Time: 35 minutes, 10 seconds

Where to Begin: The rescue helicopter finds Angus and Yellow on a log bridge over a ravine.

Where to End: Angus is being lifted to the helicopter and is assured by his rescuers that they will also get his dog.

Plot: Angus and his dog, Yellow, are stranded in the wilderness. A search plane sees them, and a rescue team drops from a helicopter to save Angus.

Review: You can use this scene to help children understand that God is like a shepherd who would give his life for the sheep. Angus finds himself in the wilderness with little hope of being rescued. Yet the rescue team is determined to find him and bring him home safely. In Psalm 23:4, the psalmist

> **The Critics Say**
> You can also use this clip to teach children about completely trusting God, Jesus rescuing us from our sin, and suffering.

> **The Critics Say**
> Kids often feel self-conscious while acting in front of their peers. You can help shy kids participate by helping groups find simple roles within the skits—roles that won't draw too much attention. Their participation will help them develop a little self-confidence. Make sure after each skit that you affirm the efforts of each group.

speaks of God's rod and staff comforting us. A shepherd uses his staff to set boundaries for the sheep, as a weapon against predators, and as a guide to get sheep to a safe place.

 Supplies: Bibles

now PLAYING

Divide the kids into three groups. Group 1 will create a skit illustrating the first two verses of Psalm 23; group 2, verses 3 and 4; and group 3, verses 5 and 6. Give kids about ten minutes to come up with their skits. Encourage groups to provide parts for each person in their skits. For example, they can act as sheep being led to the quiet waters, they can show the shepherd tending his sheep with a rod and staff, or could even be a human "house." After kids have prepared their skits, have a reader from each group, read their two verses from the Bible then present its skit for the other kids.

Say→ We're going to watch a scene from *Far From Home.* The main character is a boy named Angus who is stranded in a wilderness. In this scene he is hanging on a log bridge above a ravine.

Show the *Far From Home* clip.

Ask→ • How do you think Angus felt when the rescue helicopter hovered over him?
• What kind of trust did Angus have in his rescue team as they lifted him to the helicopter?

Say→ In Psalm 23, God is represented as the shepherd. Think back to the skits each of you created. Some of you acted as the shepherd who would give his life for the sheep. Others of you acted as the sheep who depend on God in difficult situations. In real life each of us is like the sheep. God comforts us when we're hurting, guides us through life, is with us in difficult times, gives us the things we need, and shows us mercy, even when we disobey him.

Ask→ • How is the rescue team in the movie clip like the shepherd who watches his sheep?
• What things are you sometimes afraid or fearful of?
• How can God help us overcome these fears?

HE'S MY LEADER • *Scripture: Psalm 23*

Movie Title:
ONE HUNDRED AND ONE DALMATIANS (1961) (NOT RATED)

Start Time: 30 minutes, 10 seconds

Where to Begin: Tibs, the cat, and Colonel, the dog, see a car zipping to the abandoned mansion.

Where to End: Tibs pushes the last puppy out of the abandoned mansion.

The Critics Say

You can also use this clip to teach children about friendship, God's provision, or obeying and honoring parents.

Plot: Cruella De Vil and her henchmen are holding the Dalmatians hostage in an abandoned mansion with the intent of taking their fur. The cat, Tibs, and the dog, Colonel, execute a rescue mission to free the dogs from their evil captors.

Review: You can use this clip to help children understand Psalm 23 and the way it illustrates how we should depend on God. The Dalmatian puppies are facing sure death but are rescued. Psalm 23 is a beautiful poem, showing how God protects us and rescues us from difficulty.

Supplies: Blindfolds

Preshow: Prior to class, set up an obstacle course in your room. You can use a row of chairs that the kids will have to walk around, tables for them to crawl under, a trash can the kids must step over, and carpet squares for the kids to step on.

now PLAYING

Have the children form pairs. Line partners in a row at the start of the obstacle course. Blindfold one partner. The partner with the blindfold must navigate the course with instructions from his or her partner. The two partners must not touch each other. After each blindfolded partner has gone through the course, have the partners switch so that each child has an opportunity to navigate the course.

Say→ We're going to watch a scene from *One Hundred and One Dalmatians.* Cruella has told her henchmen to get the puppies. While the bad men watch TV, Tibs rescues the puppies from the abandoned mansion.

Show the *One Hundred and One Dalmatians* clip. Then read Psalm 23.

Say→ The shepherd, God, takes care of us. In the obstacle course, you had to listen and trust the person guiding you. In the video, the puppies had to follow the directions given by Tibs. In Psalm 23, God is our guide through life.

Ask→
- What do you think the psalmist meant when he wrote, "The Lord...makes me lie down in green pastures"?
- Was it easy or difficult to follow our partners as they helped us through the obstacle course? Why?
- What will our lives be like if we let God guide our way?

> **The Critics Say**
>
> Many kids today grow up in a city or suburban atmosphere. The allusions made in the psalm to shepherds, pastures, and quiet waters may be foreign to some kids. It may be helpful before reading the psalm to read a little about the care of sheep. Use what you learn to help kids understand the metaphor of God as shepherd.

THE FIERY FURNACE

Taking a Stand • *Scripture: Daniel 3:1-30*

Movie Title:
CHARIOTS OF FIRE (PG)

Start Time: 40 minutes, 59 seconds

Where to Begin: The ship carrying the Great Britain Olympic team leaves the port.

> *The Critics Say:* You can also use this clip to teach children about obedience to God, and sharing their faith with others, or standing up for what is right.

Where to End: Eric Liddel finishes discussing his predicament of running on Sunday with the English Olympic official.

Plot: Eric Liddel is an Olympic runner from Scotland who has an opportunity to win the Gold Medal in the Olympics. When he discovers that the qualifying heat is on Sunday, he takes a stand not to run, much to the dismay of his countrymen. His decision is based on his understanding of keeping the Sabbath holy.

Review: Use this scene to help kids understand that at times we must take an unpopular stand for God. Eric Liddel was willing to sacrifice a chance at a Gold Medal in order to honor the Sabbath. In the same way Shadrach, Meshach, and Abednego refused to bow to the golden image and risked the fiery furnace.

Supplies: A Bible, chenille wires, tape

Preshow: Collect three chenille wires for each child. Prior to class, assemble a sample chenille wire standing person. Using three chenille wires, bend one chenille wire to form the legs and feet, one to form the arms, and one to form the body and the person's head.

NOW PLAYING

Show kids how to make their chenille wire people. After each child has had an opportunity to create the chenille wire person, give kids a chance to think of a way they can stand up for God. Then have kids work to make their chenille wire people stand up. Distribute tape if children are unsuccessful, and let them try again.

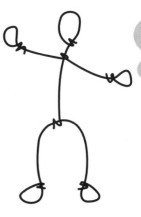

Say→ **We're going to watch a scene from *Chariots of Fire*. This is the true story of a great Scottish runner, Eric Liddel, who competed in the 1924 Olympics for Great Britain. Eric loved God and chose to obey the commandment to keep the Lord's Day holy rather than compete on Sunday.**

Show the *Chariots of Fire* clip.

Ask→
- What do you think of the stand Eric took not to run for his country on Sunday?
- How can you stand up for God?

Say→ In the book of Daniel there is a story of three men—Shadrach, Meshach, and Abednego—who chose to obey God and not bow before an idol. The penalty for disobeying was death in the fiery furnace. Read Daniel 3:13-27. God chose to spare Shadrach, Meshach, and Abednego, but the three men had stated that even if God didn't spare them they would not bow before idols.

The story of *Chariots of Fire* is a great example of standing up for God. Eventually Great Britain has Eric run in a different race that doesn't require running on a Sunday. He earns a Gold Medal. Kids will learn that God often honors us on earth if we honor him.

Ask→
- Why do you think Shadrach, Meshach, and Abednego were so brave to disobey a king and face death?
- Why do you think Eric Liddel was so willing to honor the Sabbath and face people who thought he was being a religious fool?
- How will our lives be different if we're willing to stand up for God?

I BELIEVE IN YOU • Scripture: Daniel 3:1-30

 Movie Title:
CHICKEN RUN (G)

Start Time: 1 hour, 10 minutes, 30 seconds

Where to Begin: The flying machine is wheeled out of the shed.

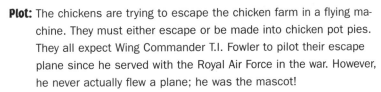

In addition to teaching about faith, this clip could also be used to illustrate the courage to defy an evil authority.

Where to End: Fowler takes control of the plane.

Plot: The chickens are trying to escape the chicken farm in a flying machine. They must either escape or be made into chicken pot pies. They all expect Wing Commander T.I. Fowler to pilot their escape plane since he served with the Royal Air Force in the war. However, he never actually flew a plane; he was the mascot!

Review: Use this scene to help children understand how important it is to have faith in God. Just as Shadrach, Meshach, and Abednego had faith that God would save them from death in the fiery furnace, Ginger had faith that Fowler could fly the plane. Unlike Fowler, however, God never hesitates to help us.

Supplies: A potato, CD or tape of children's music, and CD or tape player

NOW PLAYING

Have children sit in a circle for a variation of the game of Hot Potato. If you have a large class, form two circles. Explain that the potato is really hot, and children must pass it very quickly. Tell children that when the music stops, the person holding the potato should stand up. Start the music, let children pass the potato, encouraging speed, then stop the music. When the potato holder stands up, surprise everyone with this twist on the game. Cheer the child as a winner, saying, "Good job" and "You did great." Encourage the whole class to join in complimenting the holder of the potato. Play again a few times, giving others the chance to get the potato. Then gather everyone together and ask:

Ask→ • **How did it feel to win when you thought you were going to be out of the game if you held the potato?**
• **What was it like to have your friends tell you "good job"?**

Say→ **We're going to watch a scene from the movie *Chicken Run*. The chickens are trying to escape the chicken farm so they're not made into chicken pot pies. They've built a flying machine, and they expect old Fowler, the rooster, to fly them to safety. Let's watch.**
Show the *Chicken Run* clip.

Ask→ • **Why do you think the chickens had so much faith in Fowler?**
• **How did that give Fowler faith in himself to fly the plane?**
Briefly retell the story of King Nebuchadnezzar, and Shadrach, Meshach, and Abednego in the fiery furnace from Daniel 3:1-30. Emphasize how their faith in God saved them.

Ask→ • **How hot do you think the furnace was that Shadrach, Meshach, and Abednego were put into?**
• **Was it anything like our hot potato? Why or why not?**
• **How was Shadrach, Meshach, and Abednego's faith in God like the faith Ginger had in Fowler? How was it different?**

Say→ **God can do anything. Just as Shadrach, Meshach, and Abednego had complete faith that God would save them, we must always trust in God to protect us and trust that he loves us. One way we can do that is to pray. Let's say a prayer together.** Close with a prayer asking God to strengthen our faith in him.

DANIEL IN THE DEN OF LIONS

IF WISHES WERE PRAYERS • Scripture: Daniel 6:1-28

Movie Title:
THE GOONIES (PG)

Start Time: 59 minutes

Where to Begin: Data says, "Hey, you guys, if we keep going this far down, we'll reach China." Then the Goonies discover an underground waterfall.

Where to End: Mouth dives under the water to take back his coins.

Plot: A group of friends who call themselves "Goonies" are following an old treasure map that is rumored to lead

Use this scene to teach children to rely on prayer rather than on wishes. You can also use it to talk about greed or hurts.

to pirate treasure. They are desperate to help their families save their homes from a heartless developer. As they follow the treasure map, they stumble into the bottom of a wishing well. Stef tells the kids they can't pick up the money because each coin is someone's wish. Mouth says, "This one, this one right here, this was my dream, my wish and it didn't come true, so I'm taking it back. I'm taking them all back."

Review: Use this clip to teach children to have faith rather than rely on wishes. Mouth is upset because the wishes he made at the wishing well never came true. Daniel never relied on wishes to save him in the den of lions. Daniel prayed to God three times each day and had faith that God would protect him. True faith in God is what matters, not wishes or "good luck" charms.

Supplies: A Bible, index cards, pens, and markers or crayons

Preshow: For each child in your class, write "Wish Card" on the top of one index card and "Prayer Card" on the top of another. If children are old enough, they can do this themselves.

The Goonies is rated PG for some of the language in this film, but there is no objectionable language in this clip.

now PLaYiNG

Distribute a Wish Card and a Prayer Card to each child. Make markers available to the class.

Say→ **On your Wish Card, I want you to write or draw something that you wish for.** When everyone is finished say, **On your Prayer Card, I want you to draw or write something you would like all of us to pray for.** Take a few minutes and let kids share what they wrote or drew on their Wish Cards, but tell them not to share their Prayer Cards yet.

Let's watch a scene from *The Goonies*. The Goonies are a group of friends who are following a pirate's map to hidden treasure. Their journey is very dangerous, but they need to find the treasure to save their parents' homes from an evil man who wants to tear down all their houses.

Show the *Goonies* clip.

Ask→ • **Why do you think Mouth's wishes never came true?**
• **What's a better way to ask for something rather than making a wish?**

Have someone read aloud Daniel 6:16-23, or read the passage yourself. Before you start, explain that Daniel is going to be thrown into the lions' den because he disobeyed an order from the king not to pray to God. Then ask:

- **Did Daniel make a wish or pray to God to save him?**
- **Is praying to God better than wishing for something? Why?**
- **What's the difference between a wish and a prayer?**

Say→ **We should always rely on prayer and never on wishes or lucky charms. It's OK to wish and hope sometimes, but if you really want someone to listen, pray to God about it. He is always there to listen. God may not always give you what you want, but he knows what's best for you.**

Have each child share the request on his or her Prayer Card, and pray as a group for those requests. Encourage children to take their Prayer Cards home and share them with their families.

---

a STORY OF FaITH • *Scripture: Daniel 6:1-28*

Movie Title:
THE FOURTH WISE MAN

Start Time: 53 minutes

Where to Begin: Orontes rushes in and says, "Master, I have something to report."

Where to End: Everyone waves goodbye to Orontes and Artaban.

Plot: Artaban of Persia sets out to meet up with his fellow Magi to follow the star to find the Christ child. Because he stops to help a dying man, he misses his rendezvous, and the other three wise men leave without him. With his slave, Orontes, he spends the rest of his life searching for Jesus. After living thirty years with a colony of outcasts and lepers and serving as their doctor, Artaban hears that the Messiah is in nearby Jerusalem.

> **The Critics Say**
>
> This movie illustrates persistence and unwavering faith. The final scene of the movie is a wonderful illustration of Matthew 25:35-40, that you might use for another lesson: "Whatever you did for one of the least of these brothers of mine, you did for me (verse 40)." Artaban finally meets the risen Christ, who shows him how he has given wonderful gifts to the Lord, even though they have never met.

Review: Artaban had such faith that the Messiah had been born, he gave up great wealth and power to minister to outcasts. This clip illustrates unwavering faith in God, despite great hardship and suffering. Teach your children that nothing can come between them and God as long as they remain faithful to him.

Supplies: A Bible

Preshow: Read through the story of Daniel (Daniel 6:1-28) several times to familiarize yourself with the story.

now PLAYING

Say➔ Today we're going to hear some stories about faith in God. The faith of these men was so great that it led one man to search for Jesus all of his life and another man to be saved from a den of lions. First let's watch a scene from the movie *The Fourth Wise Man.* It's about the wise man who missed meeting up with the other three wise men in the movie and didn't get to see baby Jesus. So he spent the next thirty years trying to find Jesus.

> **The Critics Say**
>
> This was originally a made-for-TV movie, but it should be readily available in movie rental stores. You might be surprised at the well-known names in the cast. The movie stars Martin Sheen, Alan Arkin, and Eileen Brennan.

Show the clip from *The Fourth Wise Man.*

Ask➔ • Do you think you could give up everything you owned to go live with the poor while you searched for Jesus? Why or why not?

• Why do you think Artaban never gave up his search for Jesus?

Say➔ Let's hear another story about a man who had great faith in God. This story is found in Daniel, chapter 6. Show children where the story is found in the Bible. **As I tell this story, I want you to act it out.** Assign children to act out the roles of Daniel, King Darius, two of the king's people, an angel, and have the rest of the children be the lions.

Tell this story, pausing to encourage children to act out their roles.

Say➔ **Daniel was a good man, but there were evil men who didn't like him.** (Have the king's people look at Daniel and whisper to each other.) **They asked the king to make a law that anyone who prays to God and doesn't pray to the king, will be thrown into a den of lions.** (Have the king pretend to sign a proclamation, and have the lions all roar.) **Daniel was very sad, and he went to his room to pray.** (Have Daniel get down on his knees to pray.) **Daniel prayed three times a day, giving thanks to God. When the king heard that Daniel was praying to God, he had to follow his own law and have Daniel thrown into the den of lions.** (Have the king point to Daniel, then to the den of lions. Have the lions roar very loud.) **The king's people threw Daniel into the den of lions.** (Have the two people gently push Daniel into the den of lions as the lions roar. Have the angel enter the lions den and tell the lions to be very quiet.)

The king went to bed (have the king lay down)**, then he got up in the morning and went to check on Daniel. Daniel spoke from the lions' den** (have Daniel stand with the angel at his side)**, and he said, "My God sent his angel, and shut the mouths of the lions."** (The lions should be very quiet and happy.) **King Darius was so happy that Daniel was saved, he ordered everyone to worship God.** (Have Daniel and the king shake hands or hug.)

Ask→ • Would you pray if you were told not to? Why?

• Would you have faith in God to save you from danger? Why?

• How can you show your faith in God every day?

Close in prayer, asking God to give children the great faith of Daniel whenever they face trouble. Encourage children to pray every day as Daniel did.

JONAH AND THE GREAT FISH

you can Run, BUT you can'T HIDE • Scripture: Jonah 1–4

Movie Title:
POLLYANNA (NOT RATED)

Start Time: 1 hour, 54 minutes, 30 seconds

Where to Begin: The wagon drops Pollyanna off at her aunt's house.

Where to End: Aunt Polly tells the staff that Pollyanna's legs are paralyzed.

> **The Critics Say**
> This scene illustrates disobedience and that you can't hide from God or authority. The entire movie also illustrates encouragement, as one small child brings happiness to a whole town with something she calls "The Glad Game."

Plot: The orphan Pollyanna goes to live with her rich Aunt Polly, who owns almost the whole town. But Aunt Polly won't support a charity bazaar to raise money for a new orphanage. Pollyanna wants desperately to attend the bazaar and climbs down a tree outside her bedroom, disobeying Aunt Polly. To sneak back into the house, she climbs up the tree, but falls and severely injures herself.

Review: Although Aunt Polly was wrong about a lot of things, Pollyanna never should have disobeyed her. It led to a terrible accident. Use this clip to demonstrate how Jonah disobeyed God and then Jonah was swallowed by the big fish. Children need to remember the commandment to honor their parents and know that they may try to hide from their parents, but they can't hide from God.

Supplies: A blindfold

NOW PLAYING

Start off with a game called Who's Missing? Explain that one child will put on a blindfold, while you point to another child to hide in the room. If you don't have a closet or other hiding place, bring a blanket, and have that child hide under the blanket. When the child is hidden, have the blindfolded child remove the blindfold and try to guess who's missing. The class can give clues. Play the game several times.

Ask→ • Does God know everything about you? Why or why not?

• Do you think God knows when you're hiding? Why or why not?

Say➜ Let's watch a movie clip about a girl named Pollyanna, who disobeyed her Aunt Polly and sneaked out of the house.

> Show the clip from *Pollyanna.*

Ask➜ • Have you ever disobeyed your parents and had something bad happen? What happened?

Say➜ Listen to this story about a man who disobeyed God. His name was Jonah. God told Jonah to go to the city of Nineveh and preach, because the city was full of wicked people. But Jonah ran away from God and jumped on a ship. He thought he could hide from God. God sent a great storm upon the sea, and the sailors were very scared. Jonah told the sailors to throw him overboard into the sea, and that would stop the storm. So the sailors threw Jonah off the ship, and God had a giant fish swallow Jonah. He stayed inside the fish for three days and three nights. While he was inside the fish, Jonah prayed to God. God had the fish leave Jonah on dry land. This time Jonah obeyed God and went to Nineveh where he preached the Word of God.

Ask➜ • What did Jonah learn from his disobedience?
• Do you think God always knows what's best for us? Why?

JUICY CONSEQUENCES • *Scripture: Jonah 1–4*

Movie Title:
WILLY WONKA AND THE CHOCOLATE FACTORY (G)

Start Time: 1 hour, 10 minutes

Where to Begin: Willy Wonka says, "Now, over here, if you'll follow me I have something special to show you."

> **The Critics Say**
> There are many illustrations in this movie of disobedience and defying authority. Pick almost any scene during the chocolate factory tour as the kids disappear one by one for not following the rules.

Where to End: Violet is rolled off to the juicer.

Plot: Willy Wonka has given out five golden tickets for five lucky children to tour his chocolate factory. As the tour progresses, the children's bad habits or personality flaws lead them each into big trouble. In this scene, Violet chews the three-course dinner gum, even after Willy Wonka tells her not to. She blows up like a giant blueberry and has to be taken out to the juicer.

Review: Willy Wonka was looking for a good, honest child, and it appears he found rebels and spoiled brats. The children continually defy his authority and disobey his rules. Each pays for his or her disobedience when something awful happens. Jonah also chose to disobey. He disobeyed God when he told him to go to Nineveh. Disaster also struck Jonah when he was thrown overboard by the sailors and swallowed by a fish. Just as God watched Jonah and knew he disobeyed, God watches us all the time.

Supplies: Paper, scissors, and markers or crayons

Preshow: Practice making the origami fish so you can easily help children with theirs.

noW PLAYING

Say→ Today we're going to watch a scene from *Willy Wonka and the Chocolate Factory.* Pay attention to who disobeys and what the consequences are.
Show the clip from *Willy Wonka.*

Ask→ • What happened because Violet disobeyed?
• Do you sometimes disobey your parents? What happens when you do?

Say→ Let's listen to a story about a man who disobeyed God and what happened to him when he disobeyed. Retell the story of Jonah from Jonah 1–4. When you're finished, ask:

• How did God get Jonah to obey him?
• How would you feel if you were swallowed by a big fish for three days?
• Does God ever need to remind you to obey him? How does he do that?

Distribute supplies and show children how to make an origami whale or a big fish (see illustration).

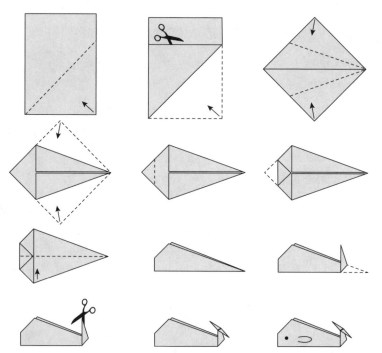

Say→ We all need to remember to obey our parents, our teachers, and others in authority. You saw what happened to Violet when she did not obey. We also need to remember to obey God. Take your big fish home to remind you to obey God. And your parents, too!

JESUS' BIRTH

a HUMBLE BEGINNING · Scripture: Luke 2:1-12

Movie Title:
A CHARLIE BROWN CHRISTMAS (G)

Start Time: 20 minutes, 30 seconds

Where to Begin: The kids look and laugh at the little tree that Charlie Brown bought.

Where to End: The kids decorate the tree and transform it.

> The Critics Say
>
> You can also use this clip to teach children about encouragement, the meaning of Christmas, or cooperation.

Plot: Charlie Brown brings a scrawny tree before the gang as the one he's chosen for the Christmas tree. The kids are disappointed at this humble, little tree. After Linus explains the true meaning of Christmas, the gang uses teamwork and all of their decorations to transform the humble tree into a beautiful one.

Review: You can use this scene to help children understand that King Jesus' coming as a baby in a manger was a very humble beginning. And like Charlie Brown's Christmas tree, his glory is revealed with time and care.

Supplies: White paper and children's scissors

Preshow: Before the children arrive, make a sample snowflake (see illustration p. 80) so that you are familiar with the steps.

noW PLAYING

Say→ We're going to watch a scene from *A Charlie Brown's Christmas.* Charlie Brown was asked to pick out a tree for the gang's pageant. Charlie Brown just brought the Christmas tree for everyone to see. Let's watch.

Play the *Charlie Brown* clip.

Ask→ • Why did the gang originally laugh at Charlie Brown's tree?
• What helped the tree get beyond its humble beginning?

Say→ Jesus came for all of us to have life here and in heaven. He came down from being king in heaven to a baby in a manger—what a humble beginning for the King of the Universe! But because he came and was born in a manger, we can know God.

Show the children a plain sheet of white paper and the beautiful sample snowflake that you made earlier. Pass out the white paper and scissors to each child, and instruct the children step-by-step in creating their own beautiful snowflakes out of plain sheets of paper.

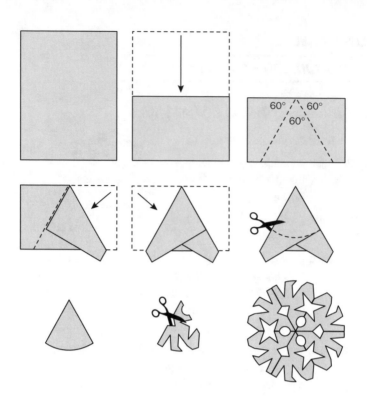

Ask➜ • How is Charlie Brown's tree or your snowflake's humble beginning like or unlike Jesus' humble beginning as a baby in a manger?

THE GREATEST TREASURE • *Scripture: Luke 2:1-12*

Movie Title:
MUPPET TREASURE ISLAND (G)

Start Time: 1 hour, 17 minutes, 40 seconds

You can also use this clip to teach children about love, selfishness, or greed.

Where to Begin: Miss Piggy is explaining where the treasure is.

Where to End: The pirates find the gold (slow motion section).

Plot: The pirates hang Kermit from the cliff and threaten Miss Piggy so she tells them where the treasure is hidden. Kermit and Miss Piggy are left hanging and sing of their love. Meanwhile, the pirates "strike it rich" with the treasure of the island.

Review: You can use this scene to help children understand the greatest treasure isn't limited to a few and isn't found in gold. The greatest treasure is found in Jesus' birth. Kermit and Miss Piggy found true love in their reunion, and the pirates found the gold treasure. Each found what they considered very valuable to them. God has given us his Son and has given us the greatest treasure. Unlike romantic love or gold treasures, the greatest treasure, Jesus, is available to anyone and everyone!

Supplies: Envelopes, small strips of colored construction paper, a small piece of foil, and candies. Be sure to have enough candy for both the "treasure" and for treats that the children can eat during the clip.

Preshow: Place a strip of colored paper in each envelope. In one envelope, put a small piece of foil. Before the children arrive, hide the envelopes around the meeting area.

The Critics Say

If you have children with food allergies, you may include non-food items like stickers for them to enjoy.

now PLAYING

Have the children hunt for all the envelopes. Have the children wait to open the envelopes. Be sure that someone has found the envelope with the foil. Gather the children together.

Say→ **Only one person has found the envelope that represents the "greatest treasure" of our hunt today—it has a piece of foil inside. Go ahead and open your envelopes, and let's find out who has it.**

Show the children all of the "treasure" candy, and give the child who found the foil the treasure.

Ask→ • **How does it feel to have worked hard at hunting and get either everything or nothing?**

Say→ **Only one person has found the "greatest treasure" of our hunt today, but we're all going to get a treat to enjoy.**

Ask the child who found the foil in the envelope to help you distribute the extra candy to the other children.

Say→ **While we enjoy the candy, we're going to watch a scene from** *Muppet Treasure Island* **where some pirates are threatening Miss Piggy and Kermit. Let's watch and see what each Muppet and pirate thinks is the greatest treasure and why.**

Show the *Muppet* clip.

Ask→ • **What did the pirates find?**
• **What did Kermit and Miss Piggy find?**

Say→ **The treasure that the pirates found was very impressive, but there is an even greater treasure that's available to all of us—Jesus! We have so much in the treasure of his birth: forgiveness, everlasting life, joy, peace, family, hope, and love. Wow! That's a treasure that no amount of gold can compare to.**

WISE MEN VISIT JESUS

IN PURSUIT • *Scripture: Matthew 2:1-12*

Movie Title:
MOUSE HUNT (PG)

Start Time: 35 minutes, 32 seconds

Where to Begin: The brothers are in the kitchen surrounded by traps, watching the mouse get a snack.

Where to End: All of the traps go off on the brothers and not one hits the mouse.

Plot: The mouse is in the kitchen making his way through a maze of mousetraps to find the perfect snack. The mouse succeeds in getting just the right snack without setting off a trap. The brothers, on the other hand, are stuck in the corner with the mouse escaping and all the traps catching them.

Review: You can use this scene to help children understand that the story of the wise men is one of pursuit. The wise men pursue Jesus because they know God's Savior has come. Herod pursues Jesus because he is threatened by this new king. God pursues a relationship with mankind by giving a Savior because of his love. In the clip, the brothers are pursuing the mouse, which is pursuing the snack.

Supplies: Apples, two or three candy bars, a large bowl or large brimmed container, and towels.

Preshow: Wash the bowl or container, fill it with water, and put the apples and candy bars in it.

> **The Critics Say**
> You can also use this clip to teach children about consequences or wisdom.

NOW PLAYING

Put the filled container in a place where all the kids can see. Ask for two or three volunteers to come dunk their heads for apples or candy bars. Remind them that they can only catch the object of their desire with their mouth or teeth. Let each volunteer try for as long as they want until they get an apple or candy bar.

> **The Critics Say**
> If you have trouble rounding up some volunteers, ask some of the adult leaders to help out! The kids will love it.

Ask➜ • How did it feel to be dunking for an apple or candy bar?

• What made you decide to keep trying or to stop trying to get what you wanted?

Say➜ When you want something badly enough you pursue, or go after, it. We're going to watch a scene from *Mouse Hunt*. The brothers are in hot pursuit of the mouse. And the mouse is in serious pursuit of a snack.

Play the *Mouse Hunt* clip.

Ask→ • What were some things that were similar and different about the brothers' pursuit and the mouse's pursuit?

• Who was successful in the pursuit?

Say→ God pursues a relationship with each one of us. God loves us so much that he sent his Son. When Jesus was born, there were many people who wanted to pursue him. Herod was jealous of Jesus and pursued Jesus to destroy him. The wise men knew that Jesus was the Savior who was promised by God. So they pursued Jesus and worshipped him by giving him gifts and praise.

Ask→ • How was Herod's pursuit like the brothers' pursuit of the mouse?

• How was the mouse's pursuit of a snack like the wise men's pursuit of Jesus?

• How can we pursue God today?

UNIQUE GIFTS • *Scripture: Matthew 2:1-12*

Movie Title:

WALLACE AND GROMIT: THE WRONG TROUSERS (NOT RATED)

Start Time: 2 minutes, 8 seconds

Where to Begin: Wallace asks Gromit if there was any post.

Where to End: Gromit crouches next to the wall as the trousers approach him.

The Critics Say

You can also use this clip to teach children about thoughtfulness or giving.

Plot: It's Gromit's birthday, and he suspects that Wallace has forgotten. Quite the contrary, Wallace has a surprise package that comes by way of their toy train. It's a very unique gift—a pair of electronic trousers. Gromit doesn't appear to understand or like his unique gift.

Review: You can use this scene to help children understand the meaning behind the unique gifts given by the wise men when they came to visit Jesus. A typical purchase for a dog is a bone or chewy toy and a typical gift for a baby is a rattle, blanket, or stuffed toy. Gromit receives a unique gift from Wallace, and Jesus receives unique gifts from the wise men—gold, frankincense, and myrrh. The wise men realized that Jesus was more than a baby born in Bethlehem—he was God's Son and the Savior of the world. So they worshipped him by giving what was valuable to them and meaningful to who Jesus was.

Supplies: Plain index cards, markers, hole punchers, ribbons and other decorating supplies, and scissors

Preshow: Cut an eight-inch ribbon for each child in your class.

now PLAYING

Hand out one index card to each child. Help the children punch two holes in their index cards close to one side and no further than one inch apart. Have them decorate their "gift" ornaments with decorating supplies. Next, string the ribbon through the holes and tie it for a neat package.

Say→ We're going to watch a scene from *Wallace and Gromit: The Wrong Trousers.* It's Gromit's birthday, and he thinks that Wallace has forgotten. Let's watch.

Play the *Wallace* clip.

Ask→ • What made Gromit's gift unique?
• What was Gromit's reaction?

Say→ After Jesus was born, some wise men came to visit him and they brought some very unique gifts. We usually think of rattles and blankets and stuffed animals as gifts for a baby's birthday, but Jesus was no ordinary baby. The wise men knew that he was God's Son and the Savior of the world—so they gave gifts that were very valuable to them and meaningful to Jesus. These wise men gave their gifts of gold, frankincense, and myrrh as ways to worship the baby Jesus.

Ask→ • What unique gift would you like to give to Jesus?
• What do you think would be Jesus' reaction?

Help any children who want to write their gifts to Jesus on their gift cards to do so.

JESUS IN HIS FATHER'S HOUSE

a MISUNDERSTANDING • *Scripture: Luke 2:41-50*

Movie Title:
VEGGIETALES: A VERY SILLY SING-ALONG (NOT RATED)

Start Time: 27 minutes, 45 seconds

Where to Begin: The song "The Pirates Who Don't Do Anything" begins.

Where to End: The song ends.

The Critics Say

You can also use this clip to teach children about confusion, laziness, or just having fun.

Plot: Larry, Pa Grape, and Mr. Lunt are lounging around singing about being pirates who don't do anything. Each verse that Pa Grape and Mr. Lunt sing is about the pirate activities that they don't do. Each verse that Larry sings is about random activities that have nothing to do with "pirate-y" things. Pa Grape and Mr. Lunt try to explain what a pirate who doesn't do anything, hasn't done. Larry "just doesn't get it." He misunderstands the point.

Review: You can use this scene to help children understand that people, including Jesus' parents, misunderstood the point of Jesus' life. When Jesus' family took a trip to Jerusalem and he was left behind, they found him in his Father's house. His parents were puzzled as to why their son was in the Temple. They misunderstood that Jesus came to do God's work of salvation by dying on the cross.

Supplies: A plate, knife, peanut butter, jam, and bread

Preshow: Set your supplies on a clean surface that can be seen by all of the children.

The Critics Say

Be sure to check for allergies before using peanut butter. You might want to have children make tuna fish, cream cheese, or turkey sandwiches instead.

NOW PLAYING

Say→ Some of you are going to help me understand how to make a peanut butter and jelly sandwich. I need you to give me some directions.

Have children each take turns giving you directions to make the sandwich. Interpret what they say literally so that you create obvious misunderstandings. For example, if a child says to put some peanut butter on the bread, scoop some out with your hand or finger and place it on the entire loaf.

Ask→ • What were you feeling when I was making the sandwich?

Say→ Misunderstandings happen all the time. We're going to watch a clip from *VeggieTales: A Very Silly Sing-Along.* The song is called "The Pirates Who Don't Do Anything." Let's watch and listen carefully. Pay close attention to the point that Larry is missing in this song.

Show the *Silly Sing-Along* clip.

Ask→ • What did Larry clearly misunderstand?
• Who was most frustrated with this misunderstanding and why?

Say→ Some misunderstandings are funny, some are frustrating, and some are tragic. When Jesus came to earth his identity was misunderstood by a lot of people—including Mary and Joseph. In fact, they misunderstood he was God's Son at least one time, when he was young and teaching in the Temple.

Jesus was here to do God's work. As Jesus grew, his earthly parents understood more about who he was and his true purpose. Jesus is still sometimes misunderstood, but now we have the Bible to tell us about Jesus and why he came.

Ask→
- How is Larry like some of the people who misunderstood or misunderstand Jesus?
- What are some ways that we can help others better understand who Jesus is?

My MISSION! • Scripture: Luke 2:41-50

Movie Title:
THE TIGGER MOVIE (G)

Start Time: 1 hour, 14 minutes, 7 seconds

Where to Begin: Tigger is sitting in the striped tree that he thinks is his family tree.

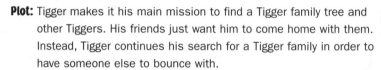

You can also use this clip to teach about persistence or family.

Where to End: The avalanche begins.

Plot: Tigger makes it his main mission to find a Tigger family tree and other Tiggers. His friends just want him to come home with them. Instead, Tigger continues his search for a Tigger family in order to have someone else to bounce with.

Review: You can use this scene to help children understand that Jesus had a mission in life. Jesus knew he must go to the Temple to be in his Father's house. Tigger had to try to find other Tiggers no matter how foolish or difficult it may have been.

Supplies: Large craft sticks, magnet strips, crayons, and all-purpose glue

now PLAYING

Say→ We're going to watch a scene from *The Tigger Movie.* Notice how Tigger is set on his mission of finding other Tiggers. See what happens when his friends find him and try to talk him into giving up his mission.

Show the *Tigger Movie* clip.

Ask→
- Is there something you have felt you needed to do, but others laughed or said it was foolish?
- Why do you think Tigger was so determined to find other Tiggers?

Say→ Tigger had a mission—he wanted to find other Tiggers. When Jesus was a boy, he understood that he had a mission, too. After his family visited the Temple, they left without knowing that Jesus had stayed behind. When Jesus' parents finally found him, he told them that he had to be in his Father's house. Jesus knew that his mission was to do what God wanted him to do.

We're going to make mission statement magnets to help us remember our mission.

Give each child one large craft stick, markers, glue, and a magnet strip. Direct children to color the craft stick with a light-colored marker for background. Direct them to write "To Know and Follow God" on the stick with a dark-colored marker. Then have the children glue the magnet strip onto the back of the craft stick.

To Know and Follow God

Say→ Take your mission statement stick home and put it on your refrigerator to help you to remember your mission in life.

JESUS IS BAPTIZED

IT PAYS TO OBEY! • *Scripture: Matthew 3:13-17*

 Movie Title:
PINOCCHIO (NOT RATED)

Start Time: 59 minutes, 59 seconds

Where to Begin: Pinocchio and Lampwick are riding the wagon that is transporting them to Pleasure Island. Lampwick is telling Pinocchio how fun it will be to be disobedient.

Where to End: Jimmny Cricket and Pinocchio run to escape Pleasure Island. Jimmny and Pinocchio jump over a cliff and into the water below.

Plot: Pinocchio and other boys are taken to Pleasure Island. On this Island children are allowed to do whatever they want. However, their disobedience leads them to becoming donkeys. Once the boys become donkeys, they are sold to Salt Mines for work. Jimmny Cricket rescues Pinocchio before he is completely transformed into a donkey.

Review: You can use this scene to reinforce the importance of obedience to God. Pinocchio learned the lesson of obedience the hard way. His choices of disobedience almost cost him his life. Through his baptism, Jesus teaches us to humbly follow God's will and to obey God's direction.

> You can use this clip to teach children about obedience to God or where sin leads.

NOW PLAYING

Say→ We're going to watch a scene from *Pinocchio*. Pinocchio and Lampwick decide to go to a place where they can disobey all the time, but their disobedience gets them into trouble. Fortunately, Jimmny Cricket steps in to help. Let's watch.

Show the *Pinocchio* clip.

Ask→
- Why do you think Pinocchio decided to be so disobedient?
- What makes you want to obey and disobey in different situations?

Say→ Jesus never sinned, but he got baptized anyway. By getting baptized, Jesus showed us that we should obey God, just as he did. Let's play a game that shows what it means to obey.

Have children stand behind a baseline at one end of the play area. Stand behind the goal line at the other end with your eyes shut and back turned to the players. Shout "Pinocchio" and count from one to ten while the players run toward you.

Shout "Jesus" and turn around. The players must stop instantly to show obedience. If you see anyone moving, that player must go back to the baseline. A player who crosses the goal line or tags you while your back is turned becomes the leader.

FOOLISH PRIDE • *Scripture: Matthew 3:13-17*

Movie Title:
LION KING II: SIMBA'S PRIDE (NOT RATED)

Start Time: 11 minutes, 14 seconds

Where to Begin: Simba warns Keara to be careful to stay inside Pride Rock and not wander away to the Outland.

> The Critics Say
> You can use this clip to teach children about obedience or pride.

Where to End: Simba scolds Keara for putting herself in danger and not obeying his warnings.

Plot: Simba, the lion king, tries to teach the young Keara how to obey him in order to protect her from danger. Keara, however, is looking for adventure and doesn't understand the gravity of Simba's instruction.

Review: You can use this scene to show that parents often give us rules in order to protect us. Keara found herself in trouble with crocodiles because she didn't obey. Even though Jesus never sinned, John baptized him in the Jordan River. By example, Jesus showed us that we need to obey God and be baptized, too!

Supplies: White construction paper, scissors, and markers

NOW PLAYING

Say→ We're going to watch a scene from *Lion King II: Simba's Pride.* Keara sends a message to her father, Simba, about her true willingness to obey him. Let's watch!

Watch the *Simba's Pride* clip.

Ask➜ • Why did Simba tell Keara to stay away from the Outland?

• Why did Keara disobey?

• What happened because of her disobedience?

Say➜ Simba gave rules to Keara to protect her. Your parents give you rules for the same reason. God gives us rules to keep us safe, too.

Give each child a piece of construction paper, scissors, and markers. Discuss traffic signs and talk about how obedience to these signs can keep drivers safe on the road.

Allow the children to create obedience signs that can rule their lives. Instruct them each to make a sign that illustrates a rule they should obey. For example, children can create a boxing glove with a line through it to show they won't fight with their brothers or sisters, make helping hands to show they'll always try to help others, or draw a mouth with sweets and smiles coming out of it to show they'll only say nice things.

Say➜ When Jesus was baptized, he gave a sign to the world that he obeyed God in everything. Let's follow Jesus' example and obey God in everything we do. Take your signs home as reminders of how important it is to obey your parents' and God's rules.

SATAN TEMPTS JESUS

THE WRONG ROAD • *Scripture: Matthew 4:1-11*

Movie Title:
TOY STORY 2 (G)

You can use this clip to teach children about temptation, peer pressure, or belonging.

Start Time: 36 minutes, 4 seconds

Where to Begin: The Round-Up Gang begins to convince Woody to go with them to Japan.

Where to End: Woody says he will join the gang and go to Japan with them.

Plot: In trying to save another toy, Woody is stolen from his home and friends by a selfish toy collector. While at the toy collector's home, Woody finds that he's part of a valuable collection of toys. The other members of the collection try to convince Woody to join them for display in a Japanese museum.

Review: You can use this scene to help children become aware of the hooks Satan uses to bait us and capture our attention away from God. Woody was tempted by the idea of fame and virtual immortality. Initially Woody went against his own best judgment. Satan tempts us by playing on our weaknesses and insecurities. However, if we follow Jesus' example and look to God's Word, we will be able to overcome temptation.

Supplies: Black or brown chenille wire, red construction paper, pencils, and children's scissors

now PLAYING

Say→ We're going to watch a scene from *Toy Story 2.* Woody is being tempted into going to Japan with the Round-Up Gang. Let's watch and see what bait the prospector uses to tempt him.

Show the *Toy Story 2* clip.

Ask→ • What bait was used to hook Woody?
• Why was it so tempting for him?
• What kinds of things tempt you?

Say→ Did you know that Jesus was tempted just as we are? Being tempted isn't sin. It's what we do with that temptation that matters. Jesus had made his mind up ahead of time that he would not take Satan's bait. God wants us to decide ahead of time that we will not take the bait. Think about the things that tempt you. Decide ahead of time not to take the bait. That will make it easier to say no!

Direct the children to draw and cut four three-inch worms from red construction paper. Allow children to write one thing on each worm that Satan has used in their life as bait. For example, children could write "cheating," "stealing," or "using bad words."

Give each child a chenille wire to bend and form a hook. Have children poke the chenille hooks through their paper worms.

Say→ Don't take the bait of Satan—he just wants to trap you. God will always be there to help us resist Satan's bait. We just need to call out to God and remember God's Word.

THE RIGHT SIDE • *Scripture: Matthew 4:1-11*

 Movie Title:
RETURN OF THE JEDI (PG)

Start Time: 1 hour, 37 minutes, 21 seconds

You can use this clip to teach children about temptation or grace.

The Critics Say

Where to Begin: Luke Skywalker has a light saber battle with the evil Darth Vader.

Where to End: Luke is tempted to join Vader but resists and instead tries to win his father back to the good side.

Plot: Luke and his friends are fighting against the dark and evil Emperor to free the galaxy from his tyrannical rule.

Review: You can use this scene to teach children that they can resist temptation and peer pressure. Luke resisted his own father who tried to get him to go to the dark side. Peer pressure can certainly be pretty overwhelming. However, God gives us the strength to overcome and do the right thing. Jesus used the Word of God to fight Satan's temptation. Luke used his sword against Vader and we can use our "swords" as well. Help children know the Word of God so they can carry their own light sabers.

Supplies: Flashlight (use a toy light saber, if available), paper, pencils, and tape

The Critics Say

This clip gives an excellent example of temptation. However, the scene is somewhat dark and frightening. Many people also feel the *Star Wars* movies include themes (such as the power of "The Force") that are connected with eastern mysticism. If you feel the children in your group will be frightened or troubled by this clip or if parents may object to the spiritual suggestions of the movie, don't show it to your class. This clip is best used with older children.

now PLAYING

Say→ We're going to watch a scene from *Return of the Jedi*. Luke is fighting off Darth Vader with his light saber. Darth Vader wants Luke to come to the dark side. Notice what Luke says to him in the clip.

Show the *Return of the Jedi* clip.

Ask→ • Do you think it was hard for Luke to resist Darth Vader's invitation to come to the dark side?
• What did Luke use to let Vader know he would not join him on the dark side?
• How can you resist Satan when he tries to tempt you?
• What weapons should we use to fight Satan?

Say→ The Word of God is like a weapon for us when we face temptation. God's Word keeps us on the right track. Jesus used God's Word when Satan tried to tempt him. Let's play a saber game to remind us to take up the weapon of God's Word.

Allow the class to look up verses about fighting temptation such as Matthew 4:10 or Proverbs 16:25 and write them out on small pieces of paper.

Tape each different verse to a flashlight or toy light saber. Divide the children into two teams. Direct each team to stand in line facing each other about eight feet apart. Assign a child on one team a corresponding number with a child on the opposite team. Place the flashlight in the center, between each team.

Call out a number, and allow the children with that number to try to grab the flashlight first without bumping into or touching the other player. The child who takes up the weapon should yell out one of the verses taped to the light.

JESUS TURNS WATER INTO WINE

TRANSFORMATION • *Scripture: John 2:1-12*

Movie Title:
INDIAN IN THE CUPBOARD (PG)

Start Time: 19 minutes, 30 seconds

Where to Begin: Omri pulls a box of toys out from under his bed.

You can also use this clip to talk about the difference between miracles and make-believe or the consequences of our actions.

The Critics Say

Where to End: Omri closes the cupboard after the toys turn to look at him.

Plot: Omri locks plastic figures inside his new cupboard with a special key. When he unlocks it, he sees that the tiny figurines have become real. He shuts the cupboard door when they stop fighting each other to look at him.

Review: You can use this clip to teach that Jesus can and still does perform miracles. Jesus' miracle shows his willingness to make the ordinary into something extraordinary.

Supplies: Kool-Aid Magic Twist, eight-ounce cups, spoons, tablespoon, and water

Preshow: Put one tablespoon of the Kool-Aid into half the cups. Put two-thirds cup of water in each of the rest of the cups.

NOW PLAYING

Give each child a spoon, a cup of water, and a cup with Kool-Aid mix.

Say→ We're going to watch a very short scene from *Indian in the Cupboard*. Omri has found out that his new cupboard can change things. He wants to see what will happen when he puts toys inside it.

Show the *Indian in the Cupboard* clip.

Ask→ • How did Omri feel when he saw his toys change?

Say→ Even though Omri didn't really make his toys real, we can see how someone reacts when he sees something unusual happen. We might feel like Omri did when *we* see God's power—excited, happy, surprised, and even scared. I want you to listen to our Bible story and think about how you would feel if you saw Jesus perform a miracle.

Read John 2:1-12.

Say→ Imagine you're a servant pouring water as Jesus asked.

Ask→ • What would happen when you pour water into your cup?

Say→ Pour water from one cup into the other cup and see if you're right. Stir it.

Ask→ • What will your drink taste like?

Say→ Try it and see. The master of the banquet didn't expect anything unusual but was surprised by the taste of the drink.

Jesus turned ordinary water into something extraordinary. It wasn't a trick like the Kool-Aid or special-effects like the movie. It was a *real* miracle. We can be grateful that miracles are real and still happen today. Jesus loves us enough to change our ordinary lives into something extraordinary.

WHO IS THIS? • *Scripture: John 2:1-12*

Movie Title:
THE SWORD IN THE STONE (NOT RATED)

Start Time: 1 hour, 15 minutes, 15 seconds

Where to Begin: The crowd walks with Arthur back to the stone.

Where to End: The crowd shouts, "Long live the king!"

The Critics Say

This scene is useful for teaching about God's power, overcoming challenges, or the importance of character.

Plot: No one believes that Arthur pulled the sword from the stone, so they go back to the churchyard to see him do it again. After the sword is replaced, others try to remove it, but only Arthur is able to do it. The people witnessing this feat proclaim Arthur king.

Review: You can connect this clip to the Scriptures by talking about how the miracles Jesus performed were one way that Jesus showed he was God's Son, just as Arthur's feat showed he was the rightful king. Jesus did not use these miracles to show off or gain power. We know that Jesus is God's Son because his miracles always helped others.

Supplies: Color-changing markers, paper

Preshow: For each child, write on a piece of paper "Jesus is God's Son" with the white color-changing marker.

The Critics Say

You can use a white crayon and colored chalk if you do not have color-changing markers.

NOW PLAYING

Hand each student the piece of paper that you've prepared.

Say→ We're going to watch part of *The Sword in the Stone*. In this scene, Arthur has told everyone that he pulled a sword out of a stone. The person who can do this is supposed to become a king. The sword was put back so that Arthur can prove that he can do it. Let's watch.

Show the *Sword in the Stone* clip.

Ask→ • Why was Arthur the only one able to pull the sword from the stone?

Say→ Let's find out what unusual task Jesus did in today's Bible story.

Read John 2:1-12.

Ask→ • Why was Jesus the only one able to perform this miracle?

Say→ In our movie, Arthur showed that he was meant to be king by what he did. He did not know who he was until that moment. Arthur also had to show his power to other people in order to become king.

Like Arthur, Jesus revealed who he was by what he did. But Jesus already knew who he was. He did not have to show his power to become God's Son. He turned water into wine not to impress people or gain power, but to help others.

Take a marker now and rub it across your paper.

Ask→ • Was this message there even when you couldn't see it?

Say→ Just like the marker helped you see the message, Jesus' miracles help us see who he is. Some people may not know about Jesus and think he is hidden from them, but he is *always* there. Like the message on our paper, the truth about Jesus has been revealed. We can tell others that Jesus is God's Son because of the many ways he has shown us his love.

MERCHANTS ARE DRIVEN FROM THE TEMPLE

TURNING THE TABLES • Scripture: John 2:13-25

Movie Title:
THE EMPEROR'S NEW GROOVE (G)

Start Time: 8 minutes, 5 seconds

Where to Begin: Pacha walks in to meet the emperor.

Where to End: Pacha is escorted out by the guards.

The Critics Say
This movie scene is also helpful when teaching about treating others with respect or about selflessness.

Plot: Emperor Kuzco tells Pacha that he intends to destroy Pacha's home to build himself a new summer palace. He doesn't care what will happen to the village that will be destroyed.

Review: You can use this scene to teach students that we shouldn't take advantage of other people, especially those who are the most vulnerable. Just as Emperor Kuzco used people for his own comfort, the Temple leaders in Jesus' day used people and their religious devotion to make money.

Supplies: A Bible, paper plates, cookies, and crackers

Preshow: Prepare one plate for each child. Put an equal number of cookies on half the plates and the same number of crackers on the other plates.

NOW PLAYING

Seat the children at tables so that each child is across from another child. Read John 2:13-25, then give one side of the table plates with cookies and the other side plates with crackers.

Say➜ I'd like you to pretend that the crackers and cookies are different types of money. If you have crackers, you are a moneychanger and if you have cookies, you are a visitor to the Temple. If you are a moneychanger, you can trade as many crackers as you want with the person across from you for cookies. If you are a visitor, you *have* to trade as many cookies as the moneychanger wants. Please trade now, but do not eat anything.

Now we're going to watch a scene from *The Emperor's New Groove.* Emperor Kuzco wants to take away Pacha's home to build another house for himself. He wants to take away Pacha's home because as emperor, he has the power to do it.

Show the *Emperor's New Groove* clip.

Ask➜ • How would you feel if you were Pacha?
• How do you feel about the trade of cookies and crackers?

Say➜ The merchants in our Bible text were a little like Kuzco. They didn't think about the visitors to the Temple in the same way that Kuzco didn't think about Pacha. They took the people's money like the way Kuzco was going to take Pacha's house, because they were in control and could do it.

Ask➜ • Who thinks we should leave our plates as they are now and eat?

Say➜ Sometimes we have to turn the tables to see how it feels to be someone else. Trade seats with the person across from you.

Ask➜ • How many of you think the plates are fair now?

Say➜ Jesus didn't like what the moneychangers had done to the people in the Temple. Jesus does not want anyone to take advantage of other people. Let's trade again until we all have an equal number of cookies and crackers. When you finish, you may eat. As you eat, remember to treat others as you would like to be treated.

SHAKE IT UP • Scripture: John 2:13-25

Movie Title:
THE HUNCHBACK OF NOTRE DAME (G)

Start Time: 25 minutes, 40 seconds

Where to Begin: Quasimodo is handed a scepter.

The Critics Say

This clip can also be used to teach about compassion for others, helping those in need, or fighting prejudice.

Where to End: Esmeralda calls for justice.

Plot: Quasimodo is crowned king of the fools, but doesn't understand that the people are mocking him. When they attack him, Esmeralda stands up to the crowd to stop them. She demands that Quasimodo be given help and that Frollo, the leader who let the crowd do this, administer justice to the situation.

Review: You can use this scene to help children understand why Jesus was upset. The crowd was mistreating Quasimodo in the same way the merchants were mistreating God's followers. The merchants had made the holiest place on earth a common market. They had lost respect for God. Jesus upset the tables to let the merchants know that their actions had upset God.

Supplies: A Bible, three large blocks, and a large ball

Preshow: In the middle of the room, set two blocks on end several inches apart and place the third across the top of those blocks to make a small table.

NOW PLAYING

Say→ It is very hard to stand up for something that is right when everyone else may be against you. In this scene from *The Hunchback of Notre Dame*, Quasimodo has been crowned king of the fools. The crowd attacks him until Esmeralda stops them.

Show the *Hunchback of Notre Dame* clip.

Ask→ • Why did Esmeralda stop the crowd?
• Why didn't anyone else try to stop the crowd?

Say→ Listen to our story to find out what Jesus was trying to stop.
Read John 2:13-25.

Say→ Let's join hands in a circle around our "table." One of you will be outside the circle with the ball. We will move around our circle to keep that person from throwing the ball into the circle and upsetting the table.

Take turns playing and then ask the children to return to their seats.

Ask→ • Why was it hard to upset the table?

Say→ There was a time when Jesus upset the tables to let people know God was upset. The merchants were used to doing business in the Temple and the people were used to being overcharged. No one seemed to see that this was wrong or wanted to change what was happening. So Jesus entered the Temple area and threw over the moneychanger's tables.

Ask→ • Why is it so hard to change something that has been wrong for a long time?

Say→ In our movie, the crowd did not respect Quasimodo. They continued to act worse and worse until someone stopped them. The merchants did not respect God or his followers. Jesus was the only one willing to stand up and say that what they were doing was wrong.

Ask→ • What are some things that God may want us to stand up against?

A GREAT CATCH OF FISH

Catching Faith • Scripture: Luke 5:1-10

Movie Title:
ANGELS IN THE OUTFIELD (PG)

Start Time: 40 minutes, 10 seconds

Where to Begin: Roger signals the manager to come over to him.

> **The Critics Say**
> This clip can be used to discuss obedience to God, persistence, or God's power.

Where to End: The batter hits the ball.

Plot: Roger wants the manager to let his team's worst batter take the place of the team's best player so that an angel can help the team win. The manager can't see angels like Roger does, but decides to do it. The worst batter is sent to the plate and hits the ball with the angel's help.

Review: You can use this scene to teach that God sometimes asks us to do impossible tasks so that we learn to trust his strength rather than our own. Peter obeyed Jesus and cast the net one last time, even though he thought it was useless to try again. We may be asked to try again and again without a "great catch," but we must keep trying. The work God gives us is meant to help us with our faith as much as it is to help others.

Supplies: String, scissors, ice cubes, water, salt, and cups

Preshow: Freeze or purchase a few ice cubes per student. Cut a six-inch piece of string, and fill a cup halfway with water for each child.

NOW PLAYING

Read Luke 5:1-10, then give each child a piece of string and a cup of water with an ice cube.

Say➜ In our story, Peter, the fisherman, listened to Jesus. I would like you to pretend you're going fishing too—ice fishing. Instead of catching fish, I want you to catch an ice cube. You may use the string as your fishing line, but don't touch the water or ice cube with any part of your body. Go ahead.

Ask➜ • How do you feel about the job I gave you?

Say➜ Peter could have chosen to give up because he thought it was too hard to try again. I'm going to ask you to try to catch an ice cube again after we watch our movie.

In this scene from *Angels in the Outfield*, Roger is asking the manager of his favorite team to replace his best player with his worst. The manager has to decide if he will to try to win with his worst player even if it seems impossible.

Show the *Angels in the Outfield* clip.

Ask➜ • How is the manager in the movie a little like Peter?

Say➜ Sometimes we are asked to do work for God that is too hard for us to do by ourselves. When we ask for God's help though, nothing is impossible. We must be willing to keep trying, even if it seems impossible.

Put a new ice cube in each cup and hand each child a spoonful of salt.

Say➜ I'm giving you a new ice cube and a spoonful of salt. I'd like you to pretend the salt is our "faith" and that we're going to add a little "faith" to our fishing. Wet the string and lay it on top of the ice cube. Pour the salt carefully on top of the string. Count slowly to ten and slowly pull the string out of the water. If your ice cube doesn't stick to the string, try again with a little more salt.

Ask➜ • What are some difficult tasks God may be asking us to try?

Say➜ Remember that through God, all things are possible. God asks us to have faith and to keep trying to do his will. Our ice fishing reminds us that even things that seem impossible can happen.

EVERYDAY MIRACLES • Scripture: Luke 5:1-10

Movie Title:
GORDY (G)

Start Time: 58 minutes, 22 seconds

Where to Begin: Hanky and Gordy are entering the barn.

Where to End: Hanky and Gordy are picked up by their traveling friends.

> **The Critics Say**
> You can also use this clip to teach children about helping one another, friends sticking together, or how God performs miracles in our everyday lives.

Plot: Hanky is helping his pig-friend, Gordy, find his family. After traveling for many miles, they realize they will need a miracle to reach their destination. Hanky explains to Gordy how miracles help us, and then they experience one.

Review: You can use this scene to help children understand how God can make the impossible possible. It seemed impossible for Gordy and Hanky to find Gordy's family and they were ready to give up. But a miracle happened when their traveling friends came by to give them a lift. When Jesus' disciples were ready to give up after a long night of fishing without a nibble, Jesus showed that God does beautiful and amazing things through miracles and helps us by making the impossible possible.

Supplies: Corn syrup, paper plates, food coloring, paintbrushes, and baby wipes

> **The Critics Say**
> It's important to help children realize that although we may want impossible things that God *can* do, God will only do the things that are best for us and accomplish his plan.

Preshow: Set out small dishes of corn syrup and several paintbrushes for children to easily share around a table covered with newspaper.

now PLAYING

Give each child a paper plate, and instruct the children to completely cover the fronts of their plates with corn syrup using the paintbrushes. Once children have finished, show them how to very carefully drip food coloring onto the syrup. Be sure to have children use baby wipes to clean their hands thoroughly when they're finished.

Say➜ You all made some beautiful and amazing paintings today! With just a couple of drops of food coloring, your plates were bursting with color. Right now we're going to watch a scene from *Gordy* and discover how sometimes beautiful and amazing things can happen in our lives. Gordy is a pig who is trying to find his family, with his friend Hanky. They need something beautiful and amazing to happen to them right about now.

Show the *Gordy* clip.

Ask➜ • How do you think Gordy and Hanky felt after talking with the big pig?
• How do you think they felt when their friends picked them up?

Say➜ Miracles are beautiful and amazing things that happen in our lives when God makes things that seem impossible...possible! When we are in need, God helps us and gives us the things we need.

Jesus performed a miracle to show the disciples how God helps us. The disciples had been fishing all night long and had caught *nothing!* They were ready to call it quits and felt very discouraged about catching any fish, just as Gordy and Hanky were discouraged about finding Gordy's folks. But Jesus told the disciples to put their nets back into the water, and "Boom!"—their nets were exploding at the seams with fish!

Remember the colors that exploded onto your plates earlier? Take your amazing artwork home with you as a reminder of how God did amazing things to help the disciples and God does amazing things to help us, too!

THE PARALYTIC IS HEALED

FRIENDS HELP FRIENDS • Scripture: Mark 2:1-5

Movie Title:
THE SECRET OF ROAN INISH (PG)

Start Time: 22 minutes, 17 seconds

Where to Begin: A woman is walking along a beach collecting food.

Where to End: The young man's eyes are opening.

You can also use this clip to teach children about selflessness, helping others, or serving God.

The Critics Say

Plot: A grandfather tells a tale of village women stumbling upon a half-drowned boy while they were searching for food near the ocean. The women take drastic measures and care to bring the young man back to good health.

Review: You can use this scene to help children understand the urgency of the paralytic's friends as they went to extreme measures to get their friend to Jesus for healing. All of us know someone who is hurting inside and that needs the power of God. Just as the paralytic's friends helped, we all should help our friends in that same way—doing whatever we can to help our friends get to Jesus. By listening to our friends, talking to them, praying for them, or even inviting them to church we can help our friends too.

Supplies: Bandages or masking tape, permanent markers, large paper grocery bags, paper lunch bags, and newspaper

Preshow: Set out all the paper bags, the markers, tape, and newspaper in an area where kids have room to work.

now PLAYING

Have the children work together to create a person from the paper bags. Guide each child in drawing a face on one side of one of the grocery bag and stuffing it with newspaper, folding over the end, and taping it closed. Then have them draw buttons down the front of another large bag, stuff it with paper, fold the end, and tape it closed. Then have each child attach the head to the torso using tape. Children can stuff the paper lunch bags to use them as arms and legs.

Say→ You all did a great job working together to put this person together. Right now we're going to watch a scene from *The Secret of Roan Inish*. The village women all worked together to help the young boy in the movie back to health by caring for him.

Show the *Secret of Roan Inish* clip.

Ask→ • How do you think the boy felt when he opened his eyes?
• How has someone cared for you when you were hurt or sick?

Say→ Hurt and sick people came from everywhere to be healed by Jesus. There was a man who couldn't walk who wanted to be healed by Jesus, so his friends went to action immediately to help him. The sick man's friends tried to carry him through the crowd to get to Jesus but there were too many people. So his friends made an opening in the roof and lowered him down to Jesus on a mat!

So many people around us are hurting and sick, often in ways we can't see on the outside. But if we share Jesus with our friends, he can help heal anything that hurts them inside. Let's all write something we would tell our friends about Jesus on a bandage. Then we'll place the bandages on our paper person we made today to remind us how Jesus can help our friends. Distribute bandages and pens.

Ask→ • How were the women in the movie like the sick man's friends?
• How can we help our friends to come to Jesus?

FAST-MOVING FEET • *Scripture: Mark 2:1-5*

Movie Title:
SHILOH (PG)

Start Time: 55 minutes, 25 seconds

Where to Begin: The dad is coming around the house carrying Shiloh.

Where to End: The boy asks if the dog is going to survive.

> **The Critics Say**
> You can also use this clip to teach children about caring for others, working together to help someone, or serving God.

Plot: Shiloh has been severely wounded in a dogfight. The entire family has to work together quickly to save Shiloh's life by getting him to the doctor. The doctor heals Shiloh due to the family's speedy reaction to a bad situation.

Review: You can use this scene to help children understand how the paralytic's friends all worked together quickly to help their friend get to Jesus to be healed. The family caring for Shiloh didn't have to take the dog to the doctor. But because they loved the dog, they worked as a team to see that the dog would be healed. When the paralytic's friends realized they couldn't get their friend through the crowd to see Jesus, they worked as a team and went to great lengths to make sure their friend would be healed.

Supplies: Permanent broad-tip markers, pairs of white socks, rubber bands, rubbing alcohol, and a spray bottle

Preshow: For each child in your class, distribute one pair of socks and several rubber bands. Set out colorful markers where children can share easily, and fill the spray bottle with rubbing alcohol and label the bottle. Before you teach children, do the craft once.

> **The Critics Say**
> Younger children may find the life or death situation with the dog scary or sad. If you feel your children may not be able to handle this suspenseful situation, don't show it to your class.

NOW PLAYING

Say→ Sometimes we have to be the hands and feet for someone else. Right now we're going to watch a scene from *Shiloh*. Shiloh has been hurt in a dogfight and can't walk. The family he's staying with has to do some fast thinking and some fast *moving*! Let's see what they do to help Shiloh.

Show the *Shiloh* clip.

Ask→ • What do you think the family was thinking when they saw that Shiloh was hurt?

Say→ God wants to help each one of us. But sometimes he works through us to help one another. We can be God's hands and feet. It's our job to help our friends get to Jesus.

People came from everywhere to be healed by Jesus. There was a man who couldn't walk to Jesus, but his friends got their hands and feet busy! They made a hole in the roof so they could lower their sick friend down to be healed by Jesus. We can help our friends who are sick or hurting by praying for them, talking to them about Jesus, or inviting them to come to church to help them know about Jesus. Whatever we do, we need to work quickly. Let's make a reminder to be God's feet for people when they need help.

Show children how to wrap their rubber bands approximately 1½" apart tightly around each sock. Demonstrate how to press the markers on the socks in various spots. Then let each child spray rubbing alcohol onto the rubber-banded socks to blend the colors. Instruct children to keep the rubber bands on the socks until they get home. Hold up a completed pair of socks.

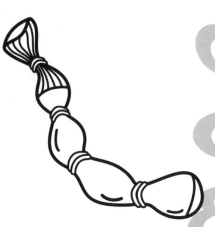

Instruct children to take their socks home, remove the rubber bands, dry the socks overnight, wash them in cold water, and dry them in a dryer. Encourage them to wear the socks as reminders that we can be God's hands and feet to help our friends get to Jesus.

THE BEATITUDES

JESUS MAKES THE BEST LEMONADE •Scripture: Matthew 5:1-12

Movie Title:
FUN AND FANCY FREE (BONGO)

You can also use this clip to teach children about peer pressure or being kind to others.

Start Time: 19 minutes, 4 seconds

Where to Begin: Bongo sees a tree and says, "Oh, boy! A tree! That's for me!"

Where to End: Bongo lies back in the flowers and says, "This is still the place for a fellow like me."

Plot: Bongo tries and tries to climb a tree to no avail. All the forest creatures make fun of Bongo and laugh at him. Still, Bongo looks on the bright side.

Review: You can use this scene to help children understand how to look forward to the promise of God's kingdom. Bongo couldn't do anything right, his friends were mean to him, and he felt all alone. But good things would come his way! Bongo could hold up his chin and rise above all the bad things going on around him because he had hope and knew those things weren't important. Bongo knew better things were to come, just as the disciples learned from Jesus.

Supplies: Ten lemons, plastic bag, a paring knife, three cups of water, two cups of sugar, four cups of crushed ice, small paper cups, a pitcher, juice press, and baby wipes

Preshow: Prepare a small piece of lemon for each child in your class. Store the lemon pieces in a plastic bag.

NOW PLAYING

Have children form a circle around you and all the ingredients listed. If you have a small group, give each child a lemon slice and see how long each child can hold the lemon slice in his or her mouth. If you have a large group, simply drip some juice on each child's washed finger to taste it.

Say→ How did that lemon taste in your mouth? Without sugar, a lemon is very sour and makes us have awful faces! Sometimes things happen in our lives that make us make awful faces too, like when we have bad days when nothing seems to go right. Let's watch a scene from *Fun and Fancy Free* and see how Bongo deals with his bad day.

Show the *Fun and Fancy Free* clip.

Ask→ • How do you think Bongo felt when nothing went right?
• What made Bongo feel better?

Say→ Jesus tells us that sometimes bad things happen. People might make fun of us. Maybe we feel like we just can't do anything right, like Bongo. But Jesus tells us *that's OK!* Things that happen to us here on earth don't matter so much when we know there are better things to come! God's preparing a special place for each one of us who love and follow Jesus. No one will ever be sad or sick or lonely. It will be *awesome.*

When things go sour like lemons in our lives or our friends' lives, we can all find joy in Jesus and in the promise of knowing one day everything will be sweet like lemonade—delicious! Let's make some right now to enjoy as a reminder of what God does with our bad situations.

Make lemonade with your group according to the following directions:

Have kids squeeze the juice out of 9½ lemons and pour the juice into a pitcher. Then have them add three cups of water and two cups of sugar. Talk about how Jesus is like the sugar in our lives—he makes the sour stuff bearable. Stir until the sugar dissolves and add four cups crushed ice. Pour into small paper cups for kids to sample.

Ask→ • **Have you ever felt how Bongo felt at the beginning? Tell about it.**
  • **How can we help others turn their "lemons" in life into "lemonade"?**

HERE COMES THE SUN • *Scripture: Matthew 5:1-12*

Movie Title:
ANNIE (PG)

You can also use this clip to teach children about patience, hope, or having a joyful heart.

The Critics Say

Start Time: 22 minutes, 12 seconds

Where to Begin: Annie is curled up in a ball in the alley.

Where to End: Annie begins walking down the street, saying, "Oh, it doesn't bother me!"

Plot: Annie is cold and feels all alone, until she meets Sandy, an orphaned dog. Annie encourages Sandy to look on the bright side of things and to have hope that tomorrow will be a better day.

Review: You can use this scene to help children understand God's promise of the kingdom to come. Annie found herself alone, destitute, and without anything in this world. But she had hope that "tomorrow" her life would be better. As Jesus spoke to the people on the mountain, he delivered that very same message that what's happening in our lives today doesn't matter so much. It's when God's kingdom comes that everything will be made perfect—and the Son will come out!

Supplies: One cup of water, food coloring, one-half cup of liquid detergent (Joy or Dawn works best), one-fourth cup of liquid starch, straw, sturdy white paper, and a large bowl

Preshow: Mix the water, detergent, starch, and several drops of food coloring together in a bowl. Use a straw to blow bubbles into the mixture.

NOW PLAYING

Have children gather around the bubble solution and hand each child a sheet of paper. Blow through a straw to create bubbles, and ask kids to think of fun or happy times that remind them of the colorful bubbles. Then have the kids lay their papers one at a time across the bowl so the bubbles pop against the paper, making a colorful print.

Say→ **Sometimes things in life happen that burst our bubbles and ruin those fun or happy times we just talked about. But good things can come from bad times, or "popped bubbles," as we discovered from the prints we just made! Let's watch a scene from *Annie* that shows how even though Annie was going through bad times, she could hold up her chin because she had hope— and she could encourage a friend along the way.**

Show the *Annie* clip.

Ask→ • How do you think Annie felt sitting in the alley?

• Why do you think she tried to encourage the dog?

Say→ Sometimes things happen that burst our bubbles. Jesus tells us that bad things will sometimes happen in our lives. But the good news is that God is there with us and he can use those bad times to do beautiful things, just like the prints we made from burst bubbles.

JESUS CALMS THE SEA

STORMY WEATHER • *Scripture: Mark 4:35-41*

Movie Title:
MARY POPPINS (NOT RATED)

Start Time: 22 minutes, 45 seconds

Where to Begin: Jane and Michael peek at the line of nanny applicants outside their door.

You can use this clip to teach children about God's power or God's plans.

Where to End: Mary rings the bell at the Banks' front door.

Plot: Jane and Michael Banks are nervous about the long line of nanny applicants that have lined up outside their home. As Jane and Michael watch, powerful winds blow the nannies away. Moments later, Mary Poppins calmly floats to the Banks' front door.

Review: The forces of nature such as wind, rain, or earthquakes, are not something that can be controlled by human effort. No wonder that Jane and Michael are amazed at the sudden changes that occur at their doorstep. They see their first clue that Mary Poppins is no ordinary nanny. When Jesus commands the winds to be still, he is revealing himself as God. The disciples watching him are amazed, and they begin to understand that Jesus is not just an ordinary man.

Supplies: A Bible, craft foam, a stapler, narrow ribbon (one-fourth inch width), paper hole punch, string, and scissors

Preshow: Cut the foam into three-inch by five-inch rectangles.

NOW PLAYING

Help the children make mini-windsocks following these instructions. Form a cylinder by holding the foam rectangle horizontally and overlapping the sides. Staple in place. Cut five ribbon strips about six inches in length. Staple the ribbons, evenly spaced, along one end of the cylinder. Punch two evenly-spaced holes at the opposite end of the cylinder. Tie a length of string through each hole and knot them together.

Say→ When you hold your windsock outside, the ribbons will fly in the direction that the wind is traveling.

Ask→ • Why is it helpful to know the direction of the wind?
• Can we do anything to change the direction of the wind or the strength of the wind?

Say→ We're going to watch a few minutes of *Mary Poppins*. In this scene, Jane and Michael Banks take a peek at the ladies who are lining up outside their door. These ladies are applying to be their nanny. From what they see so far, Jane and Michael are getting pretty nervous! Let's watch to see how Mary Poppins gets to the head of the line.

Show the *Mary Poppins* clip.

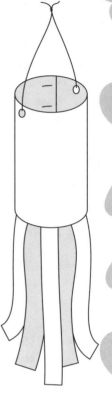

Say→ Mary Poppins may have kicked up a roaring wind and calmed it down again, but we know that in real life, controlling nature is impossible for us.

Read aloud Mark 4:35-41 from an easy-to-understand version of the Bible.

Say→ The disciples were frightened as they sailed during a raging storm, but Jesus was sound asleep! Jesus knew that the wind and the waves couldn't do anything that he wouldn't allow them to do. The disciples didn't understand at the time, but Jesus was the same God who created the wind and the waves. If he *created* them, he could easily *control* them. Jesus was using this experience to show the disciples who he really was.

CALMED DOWN • Scripture: Mark 4:35-41

Movie Title:
THE MIRACLE WORKER (1962) (NOT RATED)

Start Time: 1 hour, 37 minutes, 55 seconds

Where to Begin: Captain Keller seats Helen at the table to start her meal again.

This scene can prompt discussion about miracles, authority, communication, and independence.

Where to End: Helen touches Annie's face to feel her nod after Helen has pumped water.

Plot: Helen's family is having a welcome-home dinner for her. Early in the meal, Helen has a tantrum, and Annie attempts to correct her. Helen flings a water pitcher at Annie, and Annie takes Helen outside to fill the pitcher at the water pump. Here, for the first time, Helen relates objects to words spelled in her hand.

Review: Helen's moodiness was like the Sea of Galilee. At times she was calm, but at other times she erupted into violent tantrums. When Annie Sullivan taught Helen that things had names, and that those names could be learned by a system of hand spelling, Helen experienced a breakthrough—a "calm" in the storm of her life. Jesus calmed the sea by commanding the wind and the waters to be still. If he can calm a thunderstorm, he can surely calm the "stormy" times in our lives, too.

NOW PLAYING

Have the children scatter within the playing area. Designate one child to be "It." When the player who is "It" tags someone, he or she must say, "Quiet." Tagged players must immediately stop running and talking; they may only walk. When the player who is "It" has tagged everyone else, he or she becomes a walking player, too. The walking players attempt to tag one another, saying, "Be still." Players tagged this way must freeze in place until the end of the game. Play continues until only one player is left moving.

The Critics Say

If the weather is warm, consider playing this game outside with squirt bottles. As children run, they can squirt other players to represent "the seas." When they are tagged, the children must give up the bottles.

Ask→
- **How is the mood of our group now compared to when the game began?**
- **What changed the mood of the group?**

Say→ Sometimes we can be loud and rowdy for a good reason, but other "out of control" times can be like storms that need some calming.

Today we're going to watch a scene from *The Miracle Worker.* This is the true story of a girl named Helen who was born both deaf and blind. Just before this scene, Helen has a temper tantrum and her teacher, Annie, has tried to correct her. Helen's father tries to calm the situation, but watch to see what really helps Helen.

Play the clip from *The Miracle Worker.*

Say→ Helen finally learned that everything had a name. Learning to communicate helped Helen feel less lonely and afraid. It calmed the "storm" in her life.

Jesus used language to calm a storm, too. When he was on a boat with his disciples, a storm started to toss the boat around. The disciples were panicked, but Jesus was sleeping! Finally, Jesus awoke and commanded the wind and the waves to be still. Immediately it was smooth sailing again.

Ask→
- **When have you ever felt that something in your life was "stormy"?**
- **What can you trust Jesus to do for you when you have another "stormy" situation?**

JESUS FEEDS THE FIVE THOUSAND

KEEP 'EM COMING • *Scripture: Mark 6:35-44*

Movie Title:
THE KING AND I (G)

Start Time: 17 minutes, 33 seconds

Where to Begin: The King announces the royal children.

Where to End: Anna removes her hat, indicating her decision to stay in Siam.

Plot: Anna is disappointed to learn that the king is requiring her to live within the palace confines while she teaches his children. She begins to waver in her decision to remain, but in hopes of persuading her to stay, the king orders the royal children to meet Anna.

Review: By the end of this scene, Anna is won over. She has seen the royal children and has agreed to meet their need for education, however overwhelming the task. Similarly, Jesus agrees to meet the overwhelming need of feeding five thousand with only a handful of fish and barley loaves. God is certainly able to provide for our daily needs as well.

Supplies: Loaf of bread (enough to barely feed your class), and butter

> **The Critics Say**
> This scene may also be used to teach about respect and diversity.

> **The Critics Say**
> The children may wonder what country the king ruled. Explain that "Siam" is now called Thailand, and this musical is loosely based on a true story.

NOW PLAYING

Say→ I think we have a *need* for a snack! Let me show you how we're going to meet that need.

Show the children the loaf of bread.

Ask→ • Do you think this loaf is big enough to feed the whole class?

• Do you think it's big enough to feed five thousand people?

Say→ Let's see. Pass the loaf of bread around and let children each break off a piece.

Ask→ • Do you have enough bread for a meal?

• Do we have enough bread to feed one hundred people? one thousand people? five thousand people?

> **The Critics Say**
> This movie provides an interesting (although not entirely accurate) look at another culture. However, the movie does include songs and references to Buddhism that some parents may find objectionable.

Say→ We're going to watch a scene from a movie that takes place long ago in Thailand. A British woman named Anna has traveled there to teach the king's children. When Anna learns that she must live in the royal household she begins to have doubts. The king calls his children to meet Anna. Let's watch.

Allow the children to enjoy their snack while you play the clip from *The King and I.*

Ask→ • How do you think Anna felt when she saw so many royal children?

• Why do you think Anna agreed to stay and teach them?

Say→ Anna was introduced to all the children of the royal household. There seemed to be way too many for her to take care of. The disciples felt the same way when huge crowds of people gathered around Jesus. Jesus knew that, besides their need for food, the people had a need to know that he was God and that he could meet *all* their needs. He showed this by multiplying the little bit they had.

Jesus can do the same for us. He knows what we need before we even ask.

Ask→ • What can you trust God to provide for you?

MULTIPLYING • Scripture: Mark 6:35-44

Movie Title:
IT'S A WONDERFUL LIFE (NOT RATED)

Start Time: 55 minutes, 6 seconds

Where to Begin: George steps up to the crowd to listen to their concerns.

Where to End: The clock strikes, closing the building and loan for the day.

The Critics Say

This clip could also address issues of greed, selflessness, or compassion.

Plot: After learning that the bank has closed, panicked clients have crowded into the building and loan to withdraw money. George explains that their money has been invested in one another's property, but some clients insist on having cash. Mary offers to loan their honeymoon money, and by the end of the business day, the building and loan is left with two dollars with which to stay in business.

Review: Jesus is available to meet our needs in amazing ways. In the film, George Bailey is limited by his cash on hand, yet he loans money to everyone and ends with two dollars to spare. Jesus stretches a very limited amount of fish and bread to feed over five thousand people, with several baskets to spare. God is never limited. He is able to provide for all our needs—both physical and spiritual.

Supplies: Shoe boxes with lids, children's scissors, construction paper, tape, scissors, two colors of craft foam, large paper brads, and a pin

Preshow: Make several two-inch fish-shaped and three-inch bread-shaped stencils for the children to trace (see illustration p. 110). Cut a 1½-inch slit in the lids.

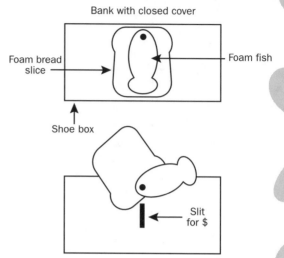

Bank with closed cover

Foam bread slice

Foam fish

Shoe box

Slit for $

Bank with open cover

Have children begin their bank projects by cutting construction paper to fit around the sides of their containers and taping the paper in place. Make the stencils available, and have the children trace the fish and bread shapes onto the craft foam and cut them out. Demonstrate how to place the fish shape on top of the bread shape and poke a brad through both pieces. Then, using a pin, poke a hole in the lid, just above the slit. Place the brad, with foam pieces, through the hole. Both pieces can be swung to the sides, revealing the slit for coins.

Say→ Some people look at the money they have in the bank to decide if their needs are met. We're going to watch a movie clip in which a bank has closed, and people are panicking because they need to have cash. They turn to a man named George Bailey for help. Let's watch.

Show the clip from *It's a Wonderful Life.*

Ask→ • How would you feel if your family had *no* money for the next week?
• How was George able to meet the people's needs?

Say→ George was able to stretch his own money—$2,000—to meet the needs of all who turned to him for help. Jesus did something more amazing when he fed the large crowds that followed him. He multiplied a few loaves and fishes to feed over five thousand people!

Unlike George, though, Jesus is never limited. He is able to provide above and beyond what we need.

Not all of our needs are physical things like food or clothing. We also need friendship, hugs, and a place to belong. Most importantly, we need a friendship with Jesus himself.

Ask→ • Can you think of ways that Jesus is already meeting your needs?
• How do you think Jesus might use *you* to meet someone else's needs?

Say→ Take your bank home with you today. When you look at the fish and the bread, remember that Jesus is able to meet your needs in amazing ways!

JESUS WALKS ON WATER

SOARING • *Scripture: Matthew 14:22-36*

Movie Title:
THE SNOWMAN (NOT RATED)

Start Time: 16 minutes, 30 seconds

Where to Begin: The snowman and the boy take a running start and begin to fly.

> The Critics Say
>
> This clip also illustrates the beauty and diversity of God's creation.

Where to End: The music ends and the snow and the boy land.

Plot: At this point in the film, the boy is having a midnight adventure with the snowman that he had made earlier in the day. While his mom and dad were sleeping, the boy brought the snowman inside to explore part of his world. Now it's the snowman's turn to show the boy the real world. With a running start, the snowman and the boy fly over countryside, oceans, and cityscapes.

Review: This scene shows an ordinary boy going along with a supernatural creature to do a superhuman feat. When Jesus does something "superhuman," however, he is revealing his divine nature. That's what was happening when he walked on water. Just as the snowman invites the boy to fly, Jesus invites Peter to try walking on water. Peter does so, but only with faith in Jesus' ability to keep him safe.

Supplies: Three paper cups per child, spoons, water, sand, sugar, and cooking oil

NOW PLAYING

Give each child three cups, and have the children fill the cups about halfway with water. Guide the children in pouring a spoonful of sand into one of the cups. Have them stir the sand and water, watching to see what will happen. Do the same with the sugar, and then the oil. The sand will sink to the bottom, the sugar will dissolve, and the oil will float.

Ask→ • **What do you notice about the way these three things interacted with water?**
• **What happens when *you* step into water?**

Say→ Most things, unless they're filled with air, will sink in water. That's why when Jesus walked on the water, he was showing that he is God. The disciples were so amazed, they thought he was a ghost! They *knew* a human couldn't walk on water. When Jesus climbed into the boat, the disciples finally realized that he truly is God.

Not only did Jesus walk on the water, but he gave someone else the same ability. Peter called out to Jesus, and Jesus invited him to walk on the water to meet him.

We're going to watch a movie clip that shows a similar situation. In this story an ordinary boy creates a snowman. During the night, the snowman comes alive and explores the boy's house. Now the snowman is going to invite the boy on an incredible journey.

Show the clip from *The Snowman*.

Ask→ • How is flying kind of like walking on water?

• Which do you think would require more faith?

• Why is it important to know that Jesus can make miracles happen?

FAITH TO FLY • *Scripture: Matthew 14:22-36*

Movie Title:
DUMBO (NOT RATED)

> You can also use this clip to illustrate confidence, faith, or overcoming obstacles.

The Critics Say

Start Time: 1 hour, 49 seconds

Where to Begin: The drumroll announces that Dumbo is about to jump from the platform.

Where to End: The end of the movie.

Plot: Dumbo knows that he can fly but up until now has relied on a feather to help him. As he jumps from the platform, he drops the magic feather and appears to be falling. With some encouragement from his mouse friend, Dumbo soars through the circus tent.

Review: When Jesus walked on the Sea of Galilee, he invited Peter to join him. Peter begins, but when he stops looking at Jesus and focuses instead on the wind and water, he begins to sink. Dumbo has a similar problem. When he drops the feather and looks around, however, fear takes over and he begins to fall. After a few words of encouragement, Dumbo changes his focus, and begins to fly around the big top.

Supplies: Masking tape and a picture of Jesus

Preshow: Make a masking-tape path across the room. Place the picture of Jesus on the wall directly above the end of the path.

NOW PLAYING

Say→ Before we watch our movie clip, we're going to conduct an experiment. We're going to see how well you can walk a straight line two different times.

Have each child take a turn walking on the line while looking only at the picture of Jesus.

Next, have all the children line up again at the starting point. This time, as they walk, they must move their head with each step they take. With the first step, they look up. With the next step, they look down; the third step, look right; the fourth step, look left. The children are to repeat this up, down, right, left pattern as they continue to walk the path.

Ask→
- Which walk was easier?
- Did you finish where you should have each time?
- What did you learn about focusing and walking?

Say→ We're going to watch a scene from *Dumbo*. In this clip, Dumbo has already learned to fly, but he's never flown in front of an audience. In fact, Dumbo thinks he can fly only with the help of a feather. This time though, he can't rely on the feather. As you watch, think about how Dumbo's focus affects his flying.

> Show the *Dumbo* movie clip.

Ask→
- When Dumbo dropped the feather, what was he focusing on?
- What changed Dumbo's focus?

Say→ In some ways flying is like walking on water. They're amazing accomplishments! When the apostles saw Jesus walk on the water, they began to understand that he truly is God. When Jesus called to Peter to join him on the Sea of Galilee, Peter got out of the boat and began walking toward Jesus. However, the Bible tells us that when Peter changed his focus—looking at the wind and waves instead of Jesus—he began to sink. Jesus had to help him stand again.

Ask→
- What things get in the way of keeping your focus on Jesus?
- What are some ways you can focus on Jesus this week?

THE TRANSFIGURATION

CHANGE FROM WITHIN • Scripture: Matthew 17:1-8

Movie Title:
BEAUTY AND THE BEAST (ANIMATED, 1991) (G)

Start Time: 1 hour, 15 minutes

Where to Begin: Belle declares her love for the Beast.

Where to End: Belle and the prince begin to dance in the ballroom.

The Critics Say

> This scene can also be used to teach about how salvation in Jesus changes us or how beauty comes from within.

Plot: Because Belle has fallen in love with the Beast before the last petal has fallen from the rose, the curse has been broken. The Beast and all the other members of the household are restored to their proper state. The Beast turns into a handsome prince, just as he was prior to the curse.

Review: During the transfiguration, Peter, James, and John get a glimpse of Jesus' true identity. They see him in glory, bringing together all the work of the law (represented by Moses) and the prophets (represented by Elijah). Jesus didn't become God during the transfiguration; he allowed the disciples to see that he was God.

Supplies: "Favorites" handouts (p. 115), and pencils

Preshow: Make a copy of the "Favorites" handout for each child.

now PLAYING

Give each child a copy of the "Favorites" handout and a pencil. Give the children a few minutes to complete the sheets. Caution the children not to discuss their answers with anyone else. Collect all the game sheets, and read aloud each one. The children should try to guess whose sheet you're reading. Continue reading until all the sheets have been identified.

Say➔ Our favorite things tell others something about us. Maybe you knew most of the answers to your best friend's list, but none of the answers to someone else's. Our personalities, our like and dislikes are something that others learn about us over time.

We're going to watch a scene from *Beauty and the Beast.* At this point in the film, Belle has looked beyond the Beast's appearance and has fallen in love with him because she has really gotten to know him. Let's see what happens next.

Play the clip from *Beauty and the Beast.*

Ask➔ • What happened to the Beast and the other members of his household?
• How do you think the prince felt to finally have Belle see him as he really is?
• How do you think Belle felt when she finally saw the Beast as a prince?

Say➔ Belle had fallen in love with the Beast—as he was on the inside. The Beast didn't *become* a prince. He had been a prince all along, though he was hidden by his beastly appearance.

When Peter, James, and John climbed a mountain with Jesus, they got to see something similar. Jesus was *transfigured,* or shown in his heavenly glory, along with Moses and Elijah. Jesus didn't *become* God at this point; he was God all along. Peter, James, and John just got a glimpse of Jesus' godly glory.

Ask➔ • Why do you think Jesus wanted these three disciples to see him in glory?
• How does it make a difference to you to know that Jesus is God?

FAVORITES

Name your favorite:

Color _____

Hobby_____

Ice cream flavor _____

Animal _____

Sport _____

Restaurant _____

Book _____

Vacation _____

Movie Title:
THE PRINCE AND THE PAUPER (ANIMATED) (G)

Start Time: 19 minutes, 55 seconds

Where to Begin: The real prince escapes from prison.

Where to End: The real prince is crowned.

> *The Critics Say*
> You can also use this movie clip to illustrate honesty or justice.

Plot: Disguised as an executioner, Goofy comes to rescue the prince from jail. Together, Goofy and the prince burst into the coronation ceremony where the prince confronts his own evil guard, Captain Pete. A zany battle takes place before Captain Pete is defeated and the prince is finally crowned.

Review: Though the prince was disguised as a beggar for a period of time, he never ceased being the prince. To many of his followers, Jesus was "disguised" simply as a carpenter's son. Though he was fully human, Jesus never ceased being God. At the transfiguration, Peter, James and John glimpsed the majesty and glory of Jesus' kingliness.

Supplies: A sheet, an assortment of dress-up clothes, including full-length robes and coats, wigs, masks, hats, dark glasses, and other disguises

> *The Critics Say*
> In this clip, the children may not realize the full impact of the prince's disguise because he is suddenly rushed to the coronation ceremony. If time allows, consider playing all of the thirty-minute video.

Preshow: Evenly distribute dress-up clothes and disguises in four areas.

NOW PLAYING

Organize the children into four teams. Explain that teams should disguise one team member from head to toe. Keep the teams separate while they are dressing their teammates.

Say→ **We're going to play Name That Player. When a disguised player from another team comes forward, other teams will take turns guessing the player's true identity.**

Give each group a sheet, and have the team members hide behind the sheet. Have each group take turns sending their disguised team member out from the sheet while others guess who he or she is.

Say→ **We're going to watch a movie clip in which a character is disguised. Watch what happens when his true identity is revealed.**

Show the clip from *The Prince and the Pauper*.

Ask→
- What were other people's reactions when the real prince entered the ceremony?
- How do you think it would feel to be mistaken for a beggar when you truly were a prince?

Say→ When Jesus came to earth, people knew he was a man, but they didn't know he was also God. The people that saw him grow up thought of Jesus as simply a "carpenter's son," and later others thought he was a great teacher or a miracle worker.

Some of the disciples that were close to Jesus were beginning to understand that although Jesus was fully man, he was also fully God. This was especially true when Jesus took Peter, James, and John with him to a mountaintop where he was *transfigured*. God allowed Peter, James, and John to catch a glimpse of Jesus' power and glory.

THE GOOD SAMARITAN

NATURAL ENEMIES • Scripture: Luke 10:25-37

Movie Title:
THE FOX AND THE HOUND (G)

Start Time: 1 hour, 14 minutes, 16 seconds

Where to Begin: The hunter looks up to see the bear.

> **The Critics Say**
>
> You can also use this scene to illustrate the themes of friendship, loyalty, or helping others.

Where to End: Tod walks out of the water and meets Copper.

Plot: Copper, the hunting hound, is sniffing out foxes for his master. Suddenly the hunter encounters a bear. Copper tries to attack the bear, but he is tossed aside. Even though he was being hunted, Tod attacks the bear from behind. Both Copper and the hunter are saved.

Review: Just before this scene, Copper has betrayed his old friend Tod. At this point in the film they are at odds— the hunted versus the hunter. In the face of danger, however, Tod risks his own life to save Copper and the hunter. This relates to a key element of the parable of the good Samaritan: an "enemy" Samaritan coming to the aid of a Jewish traveler.

> **The Critics Say**
>
> This scene will be better appreciated if you explain the background of Copper and Tod's relationship. Early in the film, an old woman takes in an orphaned Tod who quickly becomes friends with Copper. When the woman releases Tod into the woods, the two animals become estranged. They meet again when Copper is pursuing foxes for his master.

Supplies: Cleaning supplies

Preshow: Talk with the custodian of your meeting area. Ask if there is a service project for your group to do that would ease others' workload. For example, you could stack chairs, empty wastebaskets, clean nursery toys, wipe windows, or vacuum.

NOW PLAYING

Say→ We're going to watch a scene from *The Fox and the Hound.* Earlier in the film Copper, the hunting hound, and Tod the fox were best friends. Now they're grown up, and Copper is helping his master trap Tod and another fox. Watch to see what happens next.

Play the clip from *The Fox and the Hound.*

Ask→ • What surprised you about this rescue scene?
- Why do you think Tod decided to help Copper and the hunter?
- How do you suppose Copper felt about Tod after the rescue?

Say→ Foxes and hounds are usually natural enemies. They're similar to two groups of people in the Bible: the Jews and the Samaritans. Jesus told the story of a Jewish traveler who was robbed and left lying in the road. Two other Jews passed by and did not stop to help. The third person to see the traveler was a Samaritan. The Samaritan bandaged the man, took him to a nearby inn, and paid his bill. He went out of his way to help someone who was otherwise an enemy.

In both the movie clip and in the Bible story, one character saw someone else's need and decided to help. That's what we're going to do today. We're going to do a service project for someone else who uses this building.

Describe your specific service project to your group. Give assignments, based on rooms to be cleaned or tasks to be done. If it's appropriate, arrange your group in teams of four, designating one leader whose job it is to make sure the task is done correctly. Make sure that everyone has a specific task.

Ask→ • Who will be helped by the project we've just done?
- Would you have thought to help these people on any other day?
- What would help you take notice of the needs of people you see around you?

THE SAME TEAM • *Scripture: Luke 10:25-37*

Movie Title:
THE LAND BEFORE TIME V: THE MYSTERIOUS ISLAND (NOT RATED)

Start Time: 1 hour, 15 seconds

Where to Begin: Chomper's mother battles another dinosaur.

Where to End: Littlefoot's friends cheer for Chomper's rescue.

Plot: While Littlefoot and his friends look for food on an island in- habited by enemy Sharptooth dinosaurs, they become reacquainted with their friend, Chomper. During a battle, Chomper falls over a cliff and into the sea. Littlefoot endangers his own life, diving into the sea to rescue Chomper.

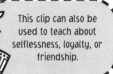

This clip can also be used to teach about selflessness, loyalty, or friendship.

Review: Littlefoot and Chomper are members of enemy dinosaur camps. In that way, they are like the Jews and Samaritans during Jesus' time. When Jesus told the story of a Jewish traveler who had been robbed, and left lying on the road, he made the hero a Samaritan. This parable teaches us the importance of showing kindness to *anyone* in need.

Supplies: Two-liter soda bottles or any narrow-necked bottles, pans of water, large serving spoons, masking tape, and a blindfold

Preshow: Fill the bottles with about 3 inches of water to keep them from tip- ping over and place a paper towel under each one. Use the mask- ing tape to mark a starting line, and station the pans and spoons across from the bottles, as you see in the diagram.

now PLAYING

Say→ **Before we watch our movie clip, we're going to play a fun relay game.**

Demonstrate how the game is played while the kids watch. Fill the serv- ing spoon with water and walk it across the room to a bottle. Carefully pour all the water into the bottle. Return to the starting line.

Say→ **Does that look easy? Well, there's going to be a little twist. Each team is going to have one team member who is handicapped in some way. It's up to each team to decide who that will be, and how that person will help their team win. Every person must be involved in this relay.**

Organize your group into four teams. Assign one of the following "handi- caps" to each group: one player is blindfolded, one player may only walk backward, one player may not use his or her hands, two players must link el- bows. Each of these players must complete the relay with his or her team.

While you play the game, take note of how each team attempts to help its handicapped teammate.

Ask→ • **How did it feel to have to play the game with a "handicap"?**
• **Did any of you attempt to help someone from *another* team? Why or why not?**

Say→ **We're going to watch a scene from *The Land Before Time V*. Watch to see how one character helps someone in need.**

Show the *Land Before Time V* movie clip.

Ask→ • **What do you think was going through Littlefoot's mind before he decided to help his friend?**

• **How do you think Chomper's mom felt about Littlefoot?**

Say→ **Chomper and the other Sharptooth dinosaurs were enemies of Littlefoot and his friends because the Sharptooth dinosaurs eat them. Even though they were supposed to be enemies, Littlefoot endangered himself to help Chomper.**

Jesus told the story of two men that were from enemy groups, too. When a Jewish traveler was robbed and beaten, a Samaritan—the enemy of the Jews—helped him. The Samaritan bandaged his injuries and paid for him to stay at an inn. Jesus told this story to teach us to serve all people—even our enemies—with love.

Room Set-Up

Starting line — pans of water with serving spoons

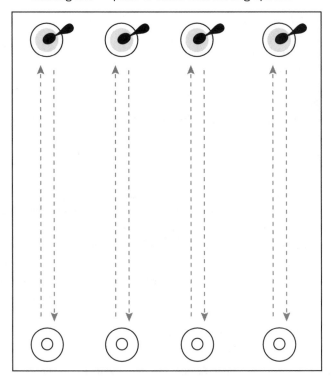

2-liter soda bottles

THE LORD'S PRAYER

TEACH US • Scripture: Luke 11:1-4

 Movie Title:
BABE (G)

You can also use this clip to teach children about cooperation, communication, or helping others.

The Critics Say

Start Time: 1 hour, 14 minutes, 35 seconds

Where to Begin: The dogs, Rex and Fly, are talking and Fly says, "If those sheep don't talk to Babe..."

Where to End: The Sheep are talking to Rex telling him they will help by giving him the password.

Plot: Babe is in trouble at the Sheepherders' contest because he can't communicate with the sheep there as he can with those at home. Rex, the dog, runs to the flock of sheep at home to learn the password that Babe needs to converse with them for the contest.

Review: Use this scene to help the children better understand how the disciples felt as they asked Jesus how to talk with God. When Babe was in trouble and needed to communicate with the sheep, Rex, the dog, went to the sheep at home. Rex needed the sheep to teach him what Babe should say to get the sheep to listen to him. We don't need a password to talk with God. We can just pray to him anytime, anywhere.

Supplies: Cotton balls and shoe boxes

Preshow: Set up two shoe boxes so that they are open and on their sides. Scatter cotton balls a few feet away from each shoe box.

NOW PLAYING

Divide the class into two teams. Give each person a cotton ball. The object is to "herd" their cotton ball sheep into the shoe box. They are to place their cotton balls just outside the line opposite the pen.

Ask→ • **If you were going to try to communicate with a sheep, what would you say? Baaaa!**

Tell the children that they are to move the cotton balls into the pen by saying "baaaa" with enough force that it moves the cotton ball. They are not to touch it with any part of their face or body. They must move each cotton ball only with their breath from the word "baaaa." Encourage teams to see how fast they can herd their sheep into the pens.

Say→ **We're going to watch a scene from *Babe*. Babe has been entered in the sheep herding competition. At home, the sheep love Babe and obediently do whatever he asks. The sheep at the competition don't know Babe and have no reason to obey the little pig's commands. Rex, the shepherd dog,**

sees that Babe is in trouble and runs to get help from the other sheep. Let's watch.

Show the *Babe* clip.

Ask➜ • Why did Babe need a password before the sheep would listen to him.

Say➜ The disciples wanted to pray to God, but they didn't know what to say. Jesus taught the disciples that they didn't need a password, they could just talk with God. Jesus told them the kind of words they could say. We call it the Lord's Prayer. The Lord's Prayer includes great ideas and words we should include in our prayers like praising God, thanking God, asking for the things we need, and asking for forgiveness.

At the end of your class, lead the children together in saying the Lord's Prayer as your closing.

JUST TALK • Scripture: Luke 11:1-4

Movie Title:
DOCTOR DOOLITTLE (1967) (G)

Start Time: 29 minutes, 45 seconds

Where to Begin: Dr. Doolittle is asking his parrot, "Could I learn to talk to animals?"

The Critics Say

You can use this movie clip to teach about communication or prayer.

Where to End: The scene changes to Dr. Doolittle in his nightshirt and he sings the phrase, "…and they could talk to me."

Plot: Dr. Doolittle has realized that he would much rather be a veterinarian than a human doctor. He also realizes that if he could converse with the animals, his job would be so much easier. He asks his parrot, who already speaks English and all the other animal languages, to teach him all the different languages that the animals speak.

Review: Dr. Dolittle wanted to communicate with the animals and realized that learning their language would help him do just that. The children in your class may want to communicate with God. Like the disciples, they may be asking, "Teach us to pray." We don't have to learn a special language to talk to God. Jesus gave the best example in the Lord's Prayer. We can teach children to go directly to God with their praise, concerns, and thanks.

NOW PLAYING

Have the kids sit in a circle. Choose one person to be the "Kitty" to begin the game. Explain to the children that Kitty has a problem and is trying to tell them about it. Kitty is to go around the circle and say "meow" to each person to try to tell them about the problem. That person must pat Kitty on the head and say three times, "Poor Kitty!" without smiling or laughing. Kitty cannot touch the person they are saying "meow" to in any way, but can say "meow" as many times as necessary. If the person patting Kitty on the head smiles or laughs before saying "Poor Kitty!" three times, they become Kitty. If they don't, Kitty moves on to the next person until someone smiles or laughs.

Say→ We're going to watch a scene from *Doctor Doolittle*. Dr. Doolittle has decided that he would rather be an animal doctor than a human doctor. He wants to help animals with their problems, but realizes that it would be so much easier if he could talk to them and find out what exactly their problems are. Let's watch.

Show the *Doctor Doolittle* clip.

Ask→ • Why did Dr. Doolittle ask his parrot to help him learn to talk to the other animals?
• What would it be like to talk to the animals?

Say→ Dr. Doolittle sort of understood the needs of his animals but realized that if he could directly communicate with them, he could help them even more. He wanted things to be even better than they were. He knew he needed to learn their language. When you were the kitty in our game, you wanted to make the person you were meowing at smile. But the only way you could talk to them was to meow. You didn't speak each other's language. There wasn't much communication.

The disciples wanted to communicate with God, but they weren't really sure how they should pray or what they should say. Jesus showed them that it wasn't too hard to pray and that they didn't have to use a special language to do it. He showed them to give God praise and thanks, to ask God to meet our needs, and to ask for forgiveness for our sins. In the Lord's Prayer, Jesus showed that we can just talk to God about these things.

THE PARABLE OF THE LOST SON

NO PLACE LIKE HOME • Scripture: Luke 15:11-32

Movie Title:
THE WIZARD OF OZ (NOT RATED)

You can use this movie clip to teach about going home to heaven or the difference between praying and wishing.
The Critics Say

Start Time: 1 hour, 36 minutes, 23 seconds

Where to Begin: Dorothy wants to go home and asks Glinda, "Will you help me?"

Where to End: Dorothy is waking up in her own bed in Kansas as she is saying, "There's no place like home."

Plot: Dorothy has been trying to find her way home after realizing that running away was a mistake. When the good witch tells her how to get home, she realizes that she could have gone home anytime. After she returns home, it's then she realizes there is no place like home.

Review: When the young man in the parable leaves home in search of a better life, it doesn't take him long to realize that there is no place like home. When he returns home, his father welcomes him with open arms. Likewise, when we become Christians, the Lord is there ready to greet us with open arms and to let us know that there is no place like home with the Lord.

 Supplies: Blindfold

NOW PLAYING

Choose a child to be "It" and another child to be "Home." While "It" is blindfolded, everyone in the class should scatter around the room. Guide the child who is Home to the opposite side of the room, and tell him or her to stay put. "It" must try to find Home while the other children try to lead him or her away from Home.

Say→ We're going to watch a scene from *The Wizard of Oz*. Dorothy has been away from home and now wants to return. She has been trying to find her way back when Glinda comes to help her. Let's watch.

Show the *Wizard of Oz* clip.

Ask→ • Have you ever been lost? How did you feel?
• When you are lost, how do you find your way home?
• Why is home such a great place?

Say→ When Dorothy ran away from home, she was sure she was going to find a life much better than the one she had. But after a little while, she realized that everything she had wanted in life was right under her nose in her own back yard.

Jesus talked about a young man who left his home. He wanted a new life, but he also learned that things were much better at home with his father. His father was there, ready and waiting for him to return.

When we sin, we are separated from our Father, God. When we finally realize that we are much better off with God in our life, he is ready and waiting for us to return to him.

Ask→ • How do you think God feels when one of us decides to "come home" and become a Christian?
• What do we have to do to "come home" to God?

NEVER ALONE • Scripture: Luke 15:11-32

Movie Title:
HOME ALONE 2: LOST IN NEW YORK (PG)

Start Time: 1 hour, 48 minutes, 20 seconds

Where to Begin: Kevin is standing in front of the Christmas tree in Rockefeller Center.

Where to End: Kevin and his mother embrace after apologizing to each other.

Plot: Kevin has run away from his family during their Christmas vacation. He now realizes how wrong he was to do so but is afraid he might never see them again. He is standing in front of the huge Christmas tree in Rockefeller Center saying what seems to be a prayer that he is very sorry for the mean things he had said about his family. He then asks if he could see his mother just one more time. At that same moment, his mother sees him and calls out to him. He apologizes to her, and she gives him a big hug.

> The Critics Say
>
> You can also use this clip to talk about family, prayer, or reuniting with loved ones in heaven.

Review: Kevin realized that he had made a terrible mistake in running away from his family. He wanted to be together with them again, but wasn't sure that they would want him back. His mother was overjoyed to see him again. Likewise, when we sin, we separate ourselves from God. When we choose to return to him, he is overjoyed and welcomes us with open arms.

> The Critics Say
>
> Some parents may object to their children viewing *Home Alone 2* as Kevin has a disrespectful attitude and there is some crude humor. If you think there may be opposition to showing this clip, don't show it to your class.

Supplies: Lemon juice, cotton swabs, white or yellow construction paper, an iron, and an ironing board or a bath towel

Preshow: Set up an ironing board, or fold the bath towel once or twice and lay it on a flat surface to iron on.

NOW PLAYING

Have the children use the cotton swabs as paintbrushes and paint an "invisible" picture on their construction paper using the lemon juice as "paint." It can be a picture of themselves with their parents or just a self-portrait. Let the pictures dry as you watch the movie clip.

Say→ We're going to watch a scene from *Home Alone 2*. Kevin has run away from his family while they are on vacation. He now realizes how wrong he was about them and that he loves them and misses them very much. Let's watch while our invisible paint dries on our pictures.

Show the *Home Alone 2* clip.

Ask→ • How do you think Kevin was feeling as he stood in front of that big Christmas tree?

• How do you think he felt when he heard his mother's voice?

Say→ When Kevin first looked at that tree, he was probably feeling very lonely and sad. He wanted nothing more than to see his mother just one more time. His mother loved him very much, and he wanted to feel the warmth of her love once again.

The Critics Say: The iron must be set on the highest setting for this to work. Take *extra caution* when ironing around the children, and only allow adult helpers to iron the pictures.

Let's take our pictures and give them some warmth and see what happens.

Take each child's picture, and iron it with a dry iron set on the highest setting. Their picture should appear before their eyes.

Summarize the parable of the lost son from Luke 15:11-32.

Say→ When we sin, we know we can always go back to God. In fact, God promises that he is always there for us. Look at your pictures. The paint never really disappeared, did it? It's the same way with God when we sin; God is always there for us. We just have to look to him to find him.

JESUS BLESSES THE CHILDREN

FAVORITE THINGS • *Scripture: Mark 10:13-16*

Movie Title:
THE SOUND OF MUSIC (NOT RATED)

Start Time: 49 minutes, 30 seconds

Where to Begin: Maria is beginning to sing to the children that have gathered in her room.

The Critics Say: You can use this movie clip to teach about fear, comfort, God's blessings, or Jesus' love for children.

Where to End: Maria explains to the captain why the children are in her room during the thunderstorm.

Plot: Maria has been hired to take care of the VonTrapp children. During a thunderstorm, they all gather in her room to be comforted. She sings to them about some of their favorite things. Their father enters the room and scolds them all for being there. Maria calmly lets the captain know that she came to comfort the children.

Review: You can use this movie clip to show how Jesus sees children. Maria valued the VonTrapp children and their feelings. When they were frightened by the storm, it was important to her to comfort them. When the captain came in and saw the children in her room, he was upset and felt they were exhibiting a lack of discipline. Maria calmly let him know that they were there because she wanted them to be. The disciples were afraid the children who were gathering around Jesus were bothering him, but Jesus let them know that he wanted them there with him.

Supplies: One unfrosted cupcake for each child, a variety of frosting and sprinkle toppings, paper plates, and plastic knives and spoons

Preshow: Put different sprinkle toppings in separate little bowls with spoons in each. Place one cupcake on a plate for each child.

> **The Critics Say**
> Make sure the kids don't think the captain is like God the Father. Rather, the captain is like the disciples, who would have the children sent away from Jesus.

NOW PLAYING

Tell children that they get to make a cupcake using some of their favorite things. Using a plastic knife, have each child frost a cupcake with a favorite flavor of frosting. Next they can choose up to three different toppings to put on their cupcakes. Children have now created their own special treats!

Say→ We're going to watch a scene from *The Sound of Music*. The children who Maria takes care of are frightened by the thunderstorm outside. She calms them down by singing a song about some of their favorite things. Let's watch.

Show the *Sound of Music* clip.

Ask→ • Why did Maria let the children stay in her room if she knew that they might get in trouble?
• How did Maria calm the children?

Say→ There are times that thinking of or having some of our favorite things makes us feel good. On our birthdays we eat our favorite kind of cake, or when we are sick or hurt, people give us gifts to make us feel better. These acts of kindness make us feel loved.

When the children came to Jesus, he wanted them to know that he loved them. The disciples didn't want the children to bother Jesus, so they tried to send the children away. This made Jesus angry because he wanted to be with the children. He told the disciples to leave the children alone. He explained to the disciples that the children were special in the eyes of God and that the disciples needed to be more like the children.

Ask→ • What do you think Jesus was talking about to the children before the disciples interrupted them?
• What do you think some of their favorite things would have been?
• What would you tell Jesus are some of your favorite things?

PART OF THE FAMILY • *Scripture: Mark 10:13-16*

Movie Title:
HOOK (PG)

Start Time: 19 minutes, 23 seconds

Where to Begin: Peter is addressing an audience of people at a banquet to honor Grandma Wendy for all her work with orphaned children.

Where to End: At the end of Peter's speech where he says, "We're all orphans."

The Critics Say

You can use this movie clip to teach about God's love or about service.

Plot: Peter and his family have come to visit Grandma Wendy and are attending a banquet being held in her honor because of all the good work she has done for orphans throughout her life. Peter is giving a speech praising her and all she had done for him as a child. Just about everyone in attendance was once a child that Grandma Wendy had "saved."

Review: Grandma Wendy loved all children. She found lost children who had no home or family and gave them the love and care that they needed. Her kindness to children can be likened to that of Jesus'. In a time when children were thought of as less important, Jesus took time to love them.

Supplies: An instant camera, white construction paper, flat lace or ribbon scraps, markers, and glue sticks

The Critics Say

If you don't have access to an instant camera, give children each a four-inch square of aluminum foil to glue on their papers shiny side up to be used as mirrors to see themselves.

Preshow: Take each child's picture as you welcome them to class.

NOW PLAYING

Say→ We're going to watch a scene from *Hook*. Peter has been asked to speak at a banquet that is honoring his adopted grandmother Wendy for all the work she has done in her life for orphaned children. Let's watch.

Show the *Hook* clip.

Ask→ • How do you think Wendy felt about the children she helped?
• How did all the people that she had helped as children feel about her?

Say→ Wendy knew that children were important. She spent her life helping children who had no place to go and no one to love them find families. Jesus also knew that children are important. He wanted to spend time with them, showing them that he loved them.

The disciples thought that the children were bothering Jesus and shouldn't be near him. When the disciples tried to make the children go away, Jesus told them to leave the children alone. Jesus said that the disciples needed to be like children if they wanted to be a part of God's kingdom in heaven. Jesus wants all children to be a part of his family.

Ask→ • How is what Wendy did for the orphaned children like what Jesus has done for us?
• How does it make you feel knowing that God wants you to be a part of God's family?

Tell the children that they are going to make their own adoption certificates to show that they can become part of God's family. Have them write the words "Let the children come to me" at the top of their certificate papers. Have children glue their instant-print pictures to the center of their certificates. Let them decorate the edges of their papers with ribbon or lace.

ZACCHAEUS

a CHANGE OF HEART • *Scripture: Luke 19:1-10*

 Movie Title:
ANASTASIA (1997) (G)

Start Time: 1 hour, 13 minutes, 55 seconds

The Critics Say

You can use this clip to teach the children about greed or about how love can change a person's heart.

Where to Begin: Dimitri enters the room where Anastasia's grandmother is. He says, "You sent for me, your grace?"

Where to End: Dimitri and Anastasia part ways as he is going down the stairs and leaving.

Plot: Anastasia's grandmother has offered a reward to anyone who can bring Anastasia to her. Dimitri and his partner have concocted a scheme to con the grandmother out of the money by having a young girl pose as Anastasia. They didn't realize that the girl they chose really was Anastasia. Dimitri has a change of heart when he is offered the money because he has fallen in love with Anastasia and realizes that it would be wrong to exploit her.

Review: At one time, Zacchaeus was a man who thought only of himself. He used other people for his own gain and money was his god. When Zacchaeus met Jesus, God's love changed his heart. He no longer sought riches, but wanted to follow Christ. Likewise, love changed Dimitri. When Anastasia's grandmother offered him his reward for finding her, he refused it stating that he had "a change of heart."

Supplies: Straws, four-inch squares of paper, colored markers, and tape

now PLAYING

Give each child two squares of paper. On one of the squares of paper, have the children draw a heart that fills as much of the square as possible. They can color them in or leave them blank. Have them write the word "Jesus" on the other square of paper. Tape the two pieces of paper to the straw so that the heart and the word "Jesus" are opposite each other with the straw sandwiched between. Take the straw and quickly spin it by rubbing your hands together with the straw in between them. When you look at the pictures, "Jesus" is now in your heart!

Say→ **We're going to watch a scene from *Anastasia*. Dimitri is finally being offered the reward that he has sought for so long. But because he loves Anastasia, he finds that he no longer wants the money. Let's watch.**

Show the *Anastasia* clip.

Ask→ • **How do you think Dimitri felt when he saw Anastasia after he left her grandmother?**

• **Why didn't he tell Anastasia that he hadn't taken the money?**

Say→ **When Dimitri decided to refuse the reward, he knew in his heart that he had done the right thing. His love for Anastasia had changed his heart, and he now desired to do what was right.**

Zacchaeus was a man who spent his life finding ways to cheat people out of their money. He thought only of himself and didn't care that his actions hurt other people. When Zacchaeus met Jesus, his heart was changed. He wanted to follow Jesus and do what was right. He gave back all the money he had taken from people. When we become Christians, our hearts change so that doing what is right becomes important for us, too.

LIKE YOU • Scripture: Luke 19:1-10

Movie Title:
THE JUNGLE BOOK (ANIMATED, 1967) (NOT RATED)

Start Time: 13 minutes

Where to Begin: Mowgli and Bagheera are just waking up after sleeping in a tree.

The Critics Say

> You can also use this clip to teach children about insecurities and how to deal with them.

Where to End: Mowgli is marching in the elephant parade, and the elephants stop. The little elephant says, "That means stop!"

Plot: Mowgli and Bagheera are sleeping in a tree. When they wake up, they can hear the elephants on patrol. Mowgli thinks it's a parade and wants to join them. He jumps down from the tree and tries to do everything that they do because he wants to be like them.

Review: From the tree, Mowgli sees the commotion of the elephants and wants to join in. Mowgli is an outsider who sees something he wants to be a part of. In the same way, Zacchaeus sees something he wants to be a part of as Jesus and his followers go by. Zacchaeus is welcomed by Jesus and quickly finds salvation.

NOW PLAYING

Say→ **We're going to watch a scene from *The Jungle Book*. Mowgli is awakened**

while sleeping in a tree when he hears the elephants on patrol. Thinking it's a parade, he wants to join in. Let's watch.

Show the *Jungle Book* clip.

Ask→ • Why do you think Mowgli wanted to join the parade?
• What did he do to try to be like them?

Say→ When Mowgli saw the elephants on parade, he wanted to be just like them.

Zacchaeus knew that there was something special about Jesus. He wanted to be with Jesus and be like Jesus. After meeting Jesus, Zacchaeus was changed forever and followed Jesus.

Have children form pairs. **I'd like you to pretend that your partner has never even heard about Jesus. I'll give you two minutes to tell your partner why you follow Jesus and why you think your partner should follow Jesus, too.**

Give children two minutes to share, then have them switch roles. Ask children to share the reasons they gave for why they follow Jesus.

JESUS ENTERS JERUSALEM

JESUS BRINGS HOPE • Scripture: Mark 11:1-11

Movie Title:
STAR WARS: THE PHANTOM MENACE (PG)

Start Time: 1 hour, 6 minutes, 25 seconds

Where to Begin: The crowd is cheering as Anakin wins the race.

The Critics Say

You can also use this movie clip to teach children about using their gifts and talents for God's glory.

Where to End: Anakin's mother is congratulating him for winning the race and says to him, "You have brought hope to those who have none. I am so proud of you."

Plot: Young Anakin Skywalker and his mother are slaves. The young slave entered in a pod race. If he wins, he will be given his freedom. The other people who were slaves look to Anakin for hope that they might someday be freed also. He wins the race and everyone rejoices. His mother congratulates him, and lets him know how proud she is of him because he has brought hope to their people.

The Critics Say

This clip gives an excellent example of a people's hero. However, many people also feel the *Star Wars* movies include themes (such as the power of "The Force") that are connected with eastern mysticism. If you feel parents may object to the spiritual suggestions of the movie, don't show it to your class.

Review: Anakin was a very common young boy. His victory brought life and hope to the common people. The common people of Jerusalem rightly saw Jesus as someone who was bringing them life and hope. They praised and worshipped him as he entered their city. Unlike Anakin, Jesus was more than just a common man, he was also God.

Supplies: Newsprint and markers, glitter glue, and other decorating supplies

NOW PLAYING

Tell the children that you are going to hold your own Hosanna Parade.

Say→ **At sporting events or parades, many people carry banners and flags to honor and praise famous or heroic people. Let's work together to make a banner or flag that welcomes, honors, and praises Jesus.**

Have children use the decorating supplies and work together to make a large banner.

Say→ **We're going to watch a scene from *Star Wars: The Phantom Menace*. Anakin Skywalker and his mother are slaves. His only hope for freedom is to win the upcoming pod race with the racing pod that he built. The race has just ended and Anakin won. Let's watch.**

Show the clip from *Phantom Menace*.

Ask→ • **How do you think the people felt as they watched Anakin win the race?**
• **How do you think his mother felt as she greeted him?**

Say→ **Anakin was a hero. He had won freedom. He had given hope to the other slaves that they might someday also be free. Jesus was bringing hope to the people of the world. He was bringing freedom from sin and hope for eternal life.**

When Jesus entered the city of Jerusalem, the people there saw a man who they knew could bring them hope and peace and they wanted to rejoice in his coming. They praised and worshipped him to let him know that they loved him.

Ask→ • **How is the way Anakin's mother felt about Anakin winning the race like the way the people felt about Jesus when he came to Jerusalem?**
• **How is it different?**
• **In what ways can we praise and worship Jesus today?**

Have children hold the banner and lead a praise parade around the room. Encourage them to shout praises as they walk around. You might also want to include noisemakers or play loud praise music.

I LOVE a PARADE • *Scripture: Mark 11:1-11*

Movie Title:
THE MUSIC MAN (NOT RATED)

Start Time: 2 hours, 27 minutes

Where to Begin: One of the proud parents stands up and shouts, "Davey, that's my Davey!"

You can also use this clip to teach children about doing their best or encouraging others.

Where to End: When the credits begin to roll.

Plot: Professor Harold Hill put together a youth band in the town of River City. When the parents saw their children actually performing, they thought the band was wonderful. They had a parade through the center of town with the professor leading the way.

Review: You can use this scene to help your children better understand the excitement that was felt in Jerusalem as Jesus entered their city. When the residents of River City saw the band that Professor Hill had put together, they were thrilled that their own children were a part of this. They wanted to honor Professor Hill with a parade to show their appreciation. When the residents of Jerusalem heard that Jesus was coming through their city, they wanted to honor and praise him with a kind of parade.

Supplies: Two nine-inch aluminum pie pans for each child, felt strips, scissors, stickers, and tacky glue

Preshow: Cut two 2x5-inch strips of felt for each child.

NOW PLAYING

Have children use tacky glue to attach the felt strips to the back of each pie pan for the handles. Then direct children to decorate the pie pans with stickers.

Say→ We're going to watch a scene from *The Music Man.* Professor Harold Hill has helped the town of River City put together a youth band. The town is so excited to see their young people working together in this marching band that they throw a parade in Professor Hill's honor. Let's watch.

Show the *Music Man* clip.

Ask→ • How do you think Professor Hill felt when he saw how happy the marching band made the people of River City?

• How would you have felt being a part of that marching band?

Say→ The people in River City used their instruments in their parade to honor Professor Hill and all he had done for their town. We can use our cymbals to honor and praise God in our own parade.

When Jesus entered the city of Jerusalem, the people were so excited to see him. They had seen and heard the many things that he had done in his ministry. They wanted him to know how much they loved and adored him. Everyone praised and worshipped Jesus as he came through town.

Lead children in a parade for Jesus. Encourage children to use their "cymbals" during the parade.

JESUS WASHES THE APOSTLES' FEET

BE A HELPER • Scripture: John 13:1-17

Movie Title:
LADY AND THE TRAMP (NOT RATED)

Start Time: 39 minutes, 58 seconds

Where to Begin: The Lady and the Tramp meet the beaver.

Where to End: The beaver gets to keep the muzzle.

The Critics Say

> You can also use this clip to help teach children about cooperation and giving.

Plot: Lady has been muzzled. She has run away from home and enlisted the aid of the Tramp for removal of the muzzle. The Tramp has taken her to the zoo for help.

Review: You can use this scene to help children understand that Jesus wants us to help others. Although the Tramp owed nothing to Lady, he wanted to help her remove the muzzle; so he helped her find a way to do it. Jesus wants us to help others regardless of who they are and what they do for us in return.

Supplies: A pitcher, a spoon, cups, powdered drink mix, and water

Preshow: Fill the pitcher with water before class, and have the other materials ready.

NOW PLAYING

Say→ We're going to watch a scene from *Lady and the Tramp*. Lady has been muzzled, and the Tramp is going to try to help her remove it. Let's watch and see if the muzzle gets removed.

Show the *Lady and the Tramp* clip.

Ask→ • Why do you think the Tramp wanted to help Lady?
• How did they get the beaver to help them?

Say→ Jesus wants us to help others. It doesn't matter who they are or what they do for us in return. Jesus wants us to have a kind spirit and help those in need. Lady was not a friend of the Tramp, but he could see that she was in trouble and needed his help. He unselfishly found a way to get her muzzle removed. Jesus washed his disciples' feet at the Last Supper to show that he wants all of us to be helpers. We spread God's love to others when we are helpers as Jesus was. Show the pitcher of water and powdered drink mix to the children.

Ask→ **Who can help me prepare a refreshing drink?** Let the children help you pour in drink mix, stir it, pour it into cups, and then pass out the cups.

Say→ **We all helped to prepare this refreshing drink. Jesus wants us to be ready to help others whenever they need it. By helping others, we are sharing God's love.**

GIVE A LITTLE BIT • *Scripture: John 13:1-17*

 Movie Title:
THE RAINBOW FISH (G)

Start Time: 7 minutes, 38 seconds

Where to Begin: The Rainbow Fish gives a scale to the Little Blue Fish.

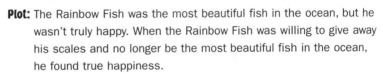
You can also use this clip to help teach children about sharing, pride, beauty, or serving.

Where to End: The Rainbow Fish begins to sing a song about sharing.

Plot: The Rainbow Fish was the most beautiful fish in the ocean, but he wasn't truly happy. When the Rainbow Fish was willing to give away his scales and no longer be the most beautiful fish in the ocean, he found true happiness.

Review: You can use this scene to help children understand a lesson that Jesus was teaching to his apostles. The Rainbow Fish was the most beautiful fish in the ocean, but he didn't find happiness until he humbled himself and gave away his scales to the fish in the ocean. Jesus humbled himself by becoming like a servant and washing the disciples' feet.

Supplies: Poster board, scissors, glue, paintbrushes, glitter, and tissue paper

Preshow: Cut one 3½x5-inch cross from the poster board for each child in your class (or have children cut them during the activity). Gather multicolored tissue paper for children to cut into squares.

now PLAYING

Give each child a cross, along with different colors of tissue paper. Show the children how to cut the tissue into squares. Then have them use the paintbrushes to glue the tissue-paper squares onto the crosses in a mosaic design and decorate the crosses with glitter. Set the crosses aside to dry.

Say→ **We're going to watch a scene from *The Rainbow Fish.* The Rainbow Fish was the most beautiful fish in the ocean, but he wasn't happy. The wise octopus told him that he must give his shiny scales away to the other fish. Let's watch and see if the Rainbow Fish gave away his scales.**
Show the *Rainbow Fish* clip.

Ask→ • **Did the Rainbow Fish want to give away his scales at first?**
• **Why do you think he changed his mind?**

Ask→ • How did the Rainbow Fish feel after he gave away his scales to the other fish?

Say→ Jesus wants us to be like the Rainbow Fish. We must be willing to give of ourselves and serve others. Jesus is the Son of God and Master of us all. He humbled himself and washed the feet of his apostles to show us that no matter how beautiful or how rich or how powerful or how great we are, we must humble ourselves and become like servants and share God's love with others.

Now I want you to be like Jesus and find someone in the class to share your cross with to show that you are willing to give of yourself to others.

THE CRUCIFIXION

NO GREATER LOVE • Scripture: Matthew 27:32-56

Movie Title:
BAMBI (NOT RATED)

Start Time: 40 minutes, 45 seconds

Where to Begin: Bambi and his mother are alone in a snowy field.

You can also use this clip to help teach children about obedience or trust.

Where to End: Bambi and the buck walk away together.

Plot: Bambi and his mother are eating in a snowy field. The mother senses danger and tells Bambi they must head for the thicket. As they run from the field, the mother sends Bambi ahead and stays behind him to make sure he is safe.

Review: Bambi's mother sensed danger and gave her own life to save Bambi's life. Jesus knew what lay ahead of him as he faced the cross, but he was willing to give his life to save ours. Jesus' love for us is even greater than the love of a mother for her child. Because of love, Jesus died for us so that we can have eternal life.

Supplies: Red construction paper, scissors, poster board, markers, tape

Preshow: Cut one 2x4-inch heart for each child (or have children cut the hearts during class). Make a 2x3-foot cross from poster board.

NOW PLAYING

Say→ We're going to watch a scene from *Bambi*. Bambi and his mother are eating in an open field. They know they must be on the alert for hunters. Let's watch.
Show the *Bambi* clip.

Ask→ • Why did Bambi's mother stay behind and let Bambi run ahead of her?
• How do you think Bambi felt when he realized his mother wasn't with him?

Say→ Jesus gave his life for us. Jesus knew how horrible the cross would be, but because of his great love for us he was willing to die so that we could live. Jesus wasn't concerned for his own safety. He knew what he had to do so we could have eternal life in heaven.

Ask→
- **How is what Bambi's mom did for Bambi kind of like what Jesus did for us?**
- **What does Jesus' dying on the cross tell us about God's love for us?**
  Give a heart to each child.

Say→ There is no greater love than the love that God has for us. **What is a way that we can share that love with other people? Write that on your heart.** After all of the children have finished, attach the hearts to the poster board cross.

HE MADE THE TRADE • *Scripture: Matthew 27:32-56*

Movie Title:
POCAHONTAS (G)

Start Time: 1 hour, 6 minutes, 26 seconds

Where to Begin: John Smith is led away to be killed.

Where to End: The chief releases John Smith.

Plot: John Smith has been captured by the Indians and is about to be put to death. Pocahontas tells her father, the chief, that if he takes the life of John Smith, he will have to take her life, too.

Review: You can use this scene to help children understand what Jesus did for us on the cross. Pocahontas was willing to trade her life to save John Smith. Jesus gave his own life so they we can have eternal life in heaven.

Supplies: Melba toast and chocolate chip cookies

> **The Critics Say**
> You can also use this clip to help teach children about forgiveness or having the courage to do the right thing.

> **The Critics Say**
> Many people feel that Pocahontas has threads of ancestor worship woven through it. Also, this scene may frighten younger children. If you feel parents may object to the frightening images or the spiritual aspects of this movie, do not show it to your class.

NOW PLAYING

Give each child a piece of Melba toast and say: **This is your snack to eat while we watch a movie clip.**

Take out a chocolate chip cookie for yourself. Just before you are about to take a bite, ask:

- **Would anyone like to trade for this cookie?** Allow all of the children to trade their Melba toast for cookies.

Say→ We're going to watch a scene from *Pocahontas* where Pocahontas is willing to trade her own life for John Smith. The chief is about to kill John Smith because of the war the Native Americans are having with the settlers. Pocahontas is running to save him. Let's watch.

   Show the *Pocahontas* clip.

Ask→ • What did Pocahontas do?
   • How do you think the chief felt about her actions?

Say→ Jesus traded his life for each of ours. He was perfect and blameless and without sin. Jesus, who did no wrong, died so all of us who sin could have eternal life with God.

Ask→ • How are the actions of Pocahontas similar to those of Jesus?
   • How are they different?

Say→ Jesus traded his life for each of ours. When you traded me for the melba toast, did you end up with a better snack? Chocolate chip cookies are much tastier than bland Melba toast, aren't they? I think that was a much better trade! Jesus' trade is the greatest trade of all. His trade allows you to have eternal life in heaven.

THE RESURRECTION

ALIVE AGAIN • *Scripture: John 20:1-21*

Movie Title:
CHARLOTTE'S WEB (G)

Start Time: 1 hour, 27 minutes, 11 seconds

Where to Begin: The spiders begin to hatch from the egg sac.

> You can also use this clip to help teach children about creation or friendship.

Where to End: Wilbur introduces Charlotte's daughters to the barn animals.

Plot: Spring has arrived and baby animals are being born. Baby spiders hatch from Charlotte's egg sac, and Wilbur is excited about their new lives.

Review: You can use this scene to help children understand the Resurrection. Although Jesus died on the cross, he rose again and lives forever. When we believe in Jesus, we have new life and will live forever as well. Charlotte had to die, but she left an egg sac full of new babies behind. Just as Charlotte gave new life, Jesus' death and resurrection give us new life, too.

Supplies: Raisins and a one-liter bottle of soda water

now PLAYING

Say→ We're going to watch a scene from *Charlotte's Web.* It's spring and new babies are being born. Wilbur is anxiously watching Charlotte's egg sac. Let's watch and see what happens.

Show the *Charlotte's Web* clip.

Ask→ • What happened to the egg sac?
• How did Wilbur feel when he saw the new spiders?

Say→ It was sad that Charlotte had died. But she gave new life when her baby spiders were born. That's kind of what happened with Jesus. It was so sad and horrible that he died on the cross. But Jesus rose from the dead. Since Jesus died and rose again, we can live with God forever in heaven. Spread the raisins on the table.

These raisins are just laying on the table—they don't have any life at all. Help me put them in this bottle. Open the soda water bottle, and have each child add a raisin to the container.

Ask→ • If we are like the raisins, how is Jesus like the soda water?

Say→ Just as the soda water seems to have given the raisins "new life," Jesus gives us new life!

NEW LIFE • *Scripture: John 20:1-21*

Movie Title:
ANNIE (PG)

Start Time: 29 minutes, 24 seconds

Where to Begin: Annie enters the mansion and meets the servants.

You can also use this clip to help teach children about love or caring for others.

Where to End: Mr. Warbucks asks, "Who are you?" and Annie replies, "I'm Annie."

Plot: Annie, an orphan girl, has been chosen to visit Mr. Warbucks and spend Christmas at his mansion.

Review: You can use this scene to help children understand that Jesus' love gives us life. When Annie first arrives at the mansion, she is warmly greeted by the servants and provided with new clothes. Quite a transformation takes place, just like what happens to our lives when we become Christians. Although we see more of an outward transformation in this clip, be sure to explain to children that Jesus brings a transformation on the inside.

Supplies: Large box with a lid, red tissue paper, scissors, plastic foam, and a knife

Preshow: Cut the red tissue paper sheets in half making sure there is enough tissue so each child can have a piece. Cut a cross from the white plastic foam. Place the cross in the bottom of a box and cover it with the lid.

NOW PLAYING

Say→ We're going to watch a scene from *Annie.* Annie lived in an orphanage. She got to visit Mr. Warbucks over Christmas. Let's watch and see what happens when she first arrives at his mansion.

Show the *Annie* clip.

Ask→ • What happened to Annie after she arrived at the mansion?
• How do you think she felt?

Say→ Annie didn't have a family. We are all kind of like Annie, until we become Christians. Then we become part of the family of God. Jesus died on the cross to save us from our sins. When we give our lives to Jesus, we join God's family and have new life.

Ask→ • How did Annie have a new life?
• How does Jesus give us new life?

Give each child a half-sheet of red tissue paper. **We all make bad choices. The bad things that we do are called sin. Pretend that this red tissue paper is your sin.** Have each child wad up the red tissue paper and throw it into the box, while you hold the box where they cannot see the cross inside.

We all sin, but Jesus takes away our sin. Carefully pull out the cross. **Jesus takes our sin away and gives us a clean heart. When we believe in Jesus, his love gives us new life.**

PENTECOST

NOW THAT'S POWER • *Scripture: Acts 2:1-13*

 Movie Title:
SUPERMAN (PG)

Start Time: 27 minutes, 18 seconds

Where to Begin: Superman's high school friends say "Bye, Clark."

Where to End: Superman is waiting for the car by the fence.

You can use this clip to help teach children about spiritual gifts or courage.

Plot: The baby, Kal-el, is sent to earth in a spaceship just before his home planet, Krypton, is destroyed. The ship lands in Smallville, Kansas, and the baby is raised by a childless couple. As the young man (now named Clark Kent) grows, he struggles to understand his destiny and how his powers are to be used. Eventually, he uses the powers to help others and becomes Superman.

Review: You can use this scene to help children understand that we have superhuman strength because we have the Holy Spirit. While we may not be able to bend steel or run faster than a bullet, we can love people when it seems hard, we can serve people when we're tired, and we can find peace when things aren't going right.

Supplies: Battery-operated flashlight

Preshow: Take the batteries out of the flashlight.

NOW PLAYING

Say→ **We're going to watch a scene from *Superman*. In this scene Clark Kent knows that he has incredible power and is trying to figure out how he should use it.**

Show the *Superman* clip.

Ask→ • **Do you think Clark Kent used his powers well or poorly in this clip?**
• **What would you do if you had that kind of power?**

Say→ **When Jesus went to heaven, God sent the Holy Spirit to help us. The Holy Spirit is more powerful than Superman or any superhero. The amazing thing is that the Holy Spirit is here to help us at anytime!**

Ask→ • **Why do you think God sent the Holy Spirit?**
• **What can the Holy Spirit help you do?**

Try to turn on the flashlight.

Say→ **I can't get this to work. Can someone else try it?** Pass the flashlight to the children.

Ask→ • **What do you think is wrong with this flashlight?** Accept all answers and keep prodding children until someone gets you to check the battery.

Open the flashlight, and show that there are no batteries. Put the batteries in, turn it on, and say: Just like the batteries give this flashlight power so it can work, the Holy Spirit gives us the power of God in our lives. The Holy Spirit probably won't give us the power to bend steel, but he will give us the power to follow God and do God's will.

SPECIAL TALENTS • *Scripture: Acts 2:1-13*

Movie Title:
AIR BUD (PG)

Start Time: 55 minutes, 31 seconds

Where to Begin: Josh and Buddy are being introduced as the halftime performance.

Where to End: Josh and Buddy look out at the crowd.

The Critics Say

You can also use this clip to help teach children about pride or spiritual gifts.

Plot: Josh has a special dog named Buddy that has an amazing talent: Buddy can shoot a basketball and make a goal.

Review: You can use this scene to help children understand that God gives us all special talents. When we allow the Holy Spirit to work in our lives, we are filled with the power of God and can do amazing things.

Supplies: Index cards, pens, large coffee can with a lid, construction paper, tape, and scissors

Preshow: Wrap construction paper around the coffee can, secure it with tape, and write "I Can" on it. Cut a slit into the lid before placing it on top. Make sure you have enough index cards so each child can have one.

NOW PLAYING

Say→ We're going to watch a scene from *Air Bud*. Josh's dog, Buddy has an amazing talent. Let's watch and see what he can do.

Show the *Air Bud* clip.

Ask→ • How did Josh and Buddy act when they performed?

• How should we act when someone recognizes our talents?

Say→ Buddy had an amazing talent! He could shoot baskets! Each of us has special talents, too—talents that are given to us from God. When we allow the Holy Spirit to work in us, we are able to do amazing things. The Holy Spirit provides us with God's power and helps us use our talents for God's glory instead of our own.

Give each child an index card. Have children write talents they have. Ask each child to share what he or she has written by saying, "I can [name of talent]," and then place the paper in the I Can container. After each child has done so, join hands in a circle around the I Can. Pray together, thanking God for sending his Holy Sprit and asking for God's help to use your talents for God's glory.

SAUL'S CONVERSION

GROWING FOR GOD • Scripture: *Acts 9:1-19*

Movie Title:
HOW THE GRINCH STOLE CHRISTMAS (1966) (NOT RATED)

Start Time: 10 minutes, 50 seconds

Where to Begin: The Whos come out and sing about Christmas.

Where to End: The Grinch carves the roast beast.

> The Critics Say
> You can also use this clip to help teach children about love, hope, salvation, or faith.

Plot: The Grinch has stolen all of the Whos' decorations and gifts. He's proud of his evil ways until he hears the Whos singing and celebrating anyway. Then his heart is warmed, and he joins the celebration.

Review: You can use this scene to help children understand the incredible power of Jesus. Saul had an evil heart just like the Grinch. Both of them wanted to stop the joy that others were feeling. When the Grinch heard the Whos singing and celebrating after he had taken away all the physical signs of Christmas, he got a new heart. After Saul's sight was restored, he got a new heart for God.

Supplies: A clean sixteen-ounce soda bottle, vinegar, baking soda, a spoon, a balloon, and a funnel

Preshow: Fill a sixteen-ounce soda bottle halfway with vinegar. Attach an un-inflated balloon to the end of the funnel, and put four spoonfuls of baking soda into the balloon.

now playing

Say→ We're going to watch a scene from *How the Grinch Stole Christmas.* The Grinch had an evil heart and didn't want the Whos to have Christmas. He has taken all of their Christmas decorations and gifts. Let's watch.

Show the *How the Grinch Stole Christmas* clip.

Ask→ • How do you think the Grinch felt when he discovered that the Whos were celebrating Christmas anyway?
• What happened to the Grinch's heart?

Say→ Jesus has the power to change people's hearts, too. In the Bible, there's a story about a man named Paul. He had an evil heart like the Grinch. Paul persecuted Christians and people that loved God. One day on the road to Damascus, God sent a strong light from heaven that blinded Paul. A man named Ananias took care of Paul until God restored his sight. When Paul was able to see again, his heart had changed. Paul then had a new heart for God.

Attach the mouth of the balloon to the neck of the soda bottle while pinching the baking soda into the top of the balloon. Be sure not to spill any of the baking soda into the bottle yet. When ready, hold the balloon up, and let the baking soda spill into the bottle. The baking soda will bubble and react with the vinegar causing the balloon to blow up. Be sure you're holding the balloon securely, or it will blow off the bottle.

Say→ Just as the balloon grew and the Grinch's heart grew, God can take an evil heart and grow it into a good heart for him.

---

a new heart • Scripture: acts 9:1-19

Movie Title:
MADELINE (PG)

Start Time: 1 hour, 21 minutes, 5 seconds

Where to Begin: Lord Covington is showing the school to its new owners.

Where to End: Madeline hugs Lord Covington and the girls cheer.

Plot: Lord Covington is showing the school to the new owners. Madeline confronts Lord Covington and asks him what his real motive is for selling the school.

You can also use this clip to help teach children about death or letting God take control.

The Critics Say

Review: You can use this scene to show children that God can change a mean and dirty heart into a clean and new one. Lord Covington had been mean to the girls. He took away their dog and had even sold their school. After listening to Madeline, his heart was changed, and he allowed the school to remain. Saul was mean to Christians. But when Jesus confronted him, Saul's heart was changed, and he became a Christian.

Supplies: Old, dirty pennies, Taco Bell's fire sauce, a bowl, and paper towels

Preshow: Collect enough pennies for each child to have one.

NOW PLAYING

Give each child a penny, and help children see that it is old and dirty. Place all of the pennies into a bowl, and pour Taco Bell "fire sauce" over them.

Say→ We're going to watch a scene from *Madeline.* Mean Lord Covington has sold the school. The girls are very upset. Let's watch and see what happens.

Show the *Madeline* clip.

Ask→ • What was Lord Covington like at the beginning of the clip?
• What made him change his heart?

Say→ Jesus can take a mean and dirty heart and change it. In the Bible, a man named Saul had a mean and dirty heart. He hurt Christians who loved God. One day Jesus appeared to Saul and his heart was changed. His mean heart became a good heart for God. Sin makes our hearts dirty, but Jesus takes away our sin and gives us clean hearts, too.

Let's look at our pennies.

Rinse off the Taco Bell fire sauce from the pennies. Dry them off with a paper towel, and pass one to each child.

Ask→ • What has happened to our pennies?
• How is that like what Jesus can do for our hearts?

Say→ Sin makes us old and dirty. Jesus can take the most dirty and evil heart and make it new for him.

MOVIE INDEX

TOPIC INDEX

Group Publishing, Inc.
Attention: Product Development
P.O. Box 481
Loveland, CO 80539
Fax: (970) 679-4370

Evaluation for
Movie Clips for Kids: Faith-Building Video Devotions

Please help Group Publishing, Inc. continue to provide innovative and useful resources for ministry. Please take a moment to fill out this evaluation and mail or fax it to us. Thanks!

● ● ●

1. As a whole, this book has been (circle one)

not very helpful   very helpful

1   2   3   4   5   6   7   8   9   10

2. The best things about this book:

3. Ways this book could be improved:

4. Things I will change because of this book:

5. Other books I'd like to see Group publish in the future:

6. Would you be interested in field-testing future Group products and giving us your feedback? If so, please fill in the information below:

Name_____

Church Name _____

Denomination _____ Church Size _____

Church Address _____

City _____ State _____ ZIP _____

Church Phone _____

E-mail _____

Exciting Resources for Your Children's Ministry

Sunday School Specials Series

Lois Keffer

This best-selling series is a lifesaver for small churches that combine age groups… large churches that host family nights…and small groups with kids to entertain. Each book provides an entire quarter of active-learning experiences, interactive Bible stories, life applications, and take-home handouts. Children love them because they're fun and you'll love the easy preparation!

Sunday School Specials	ISBN 1-55945-082-7
Sunday School Specials 2	ISBN 1-55945-177-7
Sunday School Specials 3	ISBN 1-55945-606-X
Sunday School Specials 4	ISBN 0-7644-2050-X

The Children's Worker's Encyclopedia of Bible-Teaching Ideas

You get over 350 attention-grabbing, active-learning devotions…art and craft projects…creative prayers…service projects…field trips…music suggestions…quiet reflection activities…skits…and more—winning ideas from each and every book of the Bible! Simple, step-by-step directions and handy indexes make it easy to slide an idea into any meeting—on short notice—with little or no preparation!

Old Testament	ISBN 1-55945-622-1
New Testament	ISBN 1-55945-625-6

5-Minute Messages for Children

Donald Hinchey

It's easy to share meaningful messages that your children will enjoy and remember! Here are 52 short, Bible-based messages for you to use in Sunday school, children's church, or midweek meetings.

	ISBN 1-55945-030-4
5-Minute Messages and More	ISBN 0-7644-2038-0

Just-Add-Kids Games for Children's Ministry

If your classroom is stocked with the basics (chairs, paper, a light switch and masking tape) then you've got everything you need to play dozens of great new games! You get high-energy games…low-energy games…and everything in between. Some games have Bible applications, some require no supplies at all, and every game takes just moments to explain.

ISBN 0-7644-2112-3

Order today from your local Christian bookstore, or write:
Group Publishing, P.O. Box 485, Loveland, CO 80539.

More Resources for Your Children's Ministry

Quick Children's Sermons 2: Why Did God Make Mosquitoes?

Now you're ready to answer some of the most common questions kids ask about God...Jesus...heaven...and life as they observe it. You get 50 befuddling questions straight from the lips of God's smallest saints...and great answers, too! Use this warm, witty book as a year's supply of children's sermons...for Sunday school...or to launch discussions in class or children's church!

ISBN 0-7644-2052-6

Crazy Clothesline Characters

Carol Mader

You're already familiar with these Bible stories—The Creation, Noah's Ark, Nebuchadnezzar, Jonah, Jesus' Birth, The Prodigal Son, and 34 others. But now you have 40 new and fun ways to tell them to your children! You'll tell stories with cue cards, food, walks, flashlights, balloons, and other multi-sensory items to involve children in the story...and to help them remember it for a lifetime!

ISBN 0-7644-2140-9

The Ultimate Bible Guide for Children's Ministry

You want your kids to know the difference between the Old and New Testaments. To quickly and easily find Bible verses. To understand the Bible and be comfortable exploring God's Word. Start here! These kid-friendly 5- to 15-minute activities help children from preschool through 6th grade master the skills that make Bible reading fun. Give kids a rock-solid foundation for using the Bible—and do it without boring kids.

ISBN 0-7644-2076-3

Amazing Science Devotions for Children's Ministry

Kids love figuring out how stuff works, so put their natural curiosity to work! From "What makes popcorn pop?" to "Where do rainbows come from?," here's tons of science fun that connects kids with God's wonderful world. For children's sermons...Sunday school...midweek programs and clubs...anywhere you want to give kids' faith a boost and help them learn about God!

ISBN 0-7644-2105-0